W9-AVM-184

THE WORLD OF MYTHOLOGY

EGYPTIAN MYTH

A TREASURY OF LEGENDS, ART, AND HISTORY

First published in North America in 2008 by M.E. Sharpe, Inc.

Sharpe Focus
An imprint of M.E. Sharpe, Inc.
80 Business Park Drive
Armonk, NY 10504
www.mesharpe.com

Copyright © 2008 Marshall Editions
A Marshall Edition
Conceived, edited, and designed by Marshall Editions
The Old Brewery, 6 Blundell Street, London N7 9BH, U.K.
www.quarto.com

Library of Congress Cataloging-in-Publication Data

Kramer, Ann, 1946-
  Egyptian myth : a treasury of legends, art, and history / Ann Kramer.
      p. cm. -- (The world of mythology)
  Includes bibliographical references and index.
    ISBN 978-0-7656-8105-8 (hardcover : alk. paper)
  1. Mythology, Egyptian--Juvenile literature. 2. Legends--Egypt--Juvenile
literature. 3. Art--Egypt--Juvenile literature. 4. Egypt--History--Juvenile literature. I. Title.

BL2441.3.K73 2008
299'.3113--dc22
                                    2007005876

Originated in Hong Kong by Modern Age
Printed and bound in China by Midas Printing Limited

10 9 8 7 6 5 4 3 2 1

Publisher: Richard Green
Commissioning editor: Claudia Martin
Art direction: Ivo Marloh
Picture manager: Veneta Bullen
Design and editorial: Tall Tree Ltd.
Production: Nikki Ingram

Previous page: The temple of Kom Ombo was dedicated to the crocodile god Sobek and the falcon-headed god Haroeris, also known as Horus the Elder.
Opposite: The god Amun sits on a throne protecting the pharaoh Tutankhamun
(1333–1324 B.C.E.). Amun wears two plumes on his head, symbolizing the lands of Upper and Lower Egypt.
This page and opposite: A temple dedicated to the great god Amun stands at the center of the temple complex of Karnak, begun in the sixteenth century B.C.E.

THE WORLD OF MYTHOLOGY

EGYPTIAN MYTH

A TREASURY OF LEGENDS, ART, AND HISTORY

ANN KRAMER

Sharpe Focus
an imprint of M.E. Sharpe, Inc.

CONTENTS

PHARAOHS AND GODS

MAGICAL STORIES AND LEGENDS

INTRODUCTION

The myths of ancient Egypt are among the oldest in the world. Written down by scribes and priests, they date back at least 5,000 years. Myths are stories about supernatural beings, and Egyptian myths are about their gods. These stories provide a vital insight into the Egyptians' religious beliefs and the Egyptian way of life.

The ancient Egyptian civilization has a history that spans millennia. From about 5500 B.C.E., there were farming communities around the Nile River. Two separate kingdoms emerged: Lower Egypt in the north and Upper Egypt in the south. In about 3100 B.C.E., Pharaoh Narmer united the two kingdoms, creating what was then the wealthiest and most powerful state in the world. After Narmer, pharaohs ruled Egypt for 3,000 years until, in 30 B.C.E., Egypt became part of the Roman Empire. Historians divide pharaohs into dynasties or groups, and Egypt's history into the Old, Middle, and New Kingdoms.

GIFT OF THE GODS

Egypt is a hot, dry country. The Nile River, which runs through the center, provides water, fertile soil, food, transport, and materials for building. The Greek historian Herodotus (c. 484–c. 425 B.C.E.) said Egypt was the gift of the Nile, and the Egyptians believed the Nile was a gift from the gods. The river was the lifeblood of Egypt and there would have been no civilization there without it.

Every year the Nile swelled and flooded the surrounding land in what was called the inundation. When the floodwaters receded, they left behind a deposit of rich black silt, which gave ancient Egypt its name, Kemet, the "Black Land." The river teemed with fish, and boats traveled up and down it, carrying people and goods. Either side of the Nile was a vast expanse of desert where little grew and few people lived. The desert was a hostile area, and full of dangerous animals, but it was also rich in minerals.

A SOPHISTICATED CULTURE

Ancient Egypt was a sophisticated, wealthy, and stable culture. The pharaoh, or king, ruled the country. Egyptians believed in divine kingship: that their pharaohs were divine beings, chosen by the gods. Below the pharaoh were court officials, priests, scribes, civil servants, merchants, soldiers, skilled workers, farmers, entertainers, and slaves.

The Egyptians developed one of the first writing systems, in around 3200 B.C.E. It used a complex system of pictures and symbols called hieroglyphs. Professional writers called scribes wrote on papyrus, a paper-like material made from reeds found on the banks of the Nile. The Egyptians were also great builders and engineers who constructed pyramids, temples, and other monuments to their gods and pharaohs.

Ancient Egyptians worshipped hundreds of gods—we may never know exactly how many. They believed gods had created the universe and controlled every aspect of their lives. For the Egyptians, the world could be a dangerous and unpredictable place: if the sun did not shine, or if the Nile did not flood, there would be chaos. They looked to their gods to ensure order and stability.

Sun worship was a major part of Egyptian religion, but ideas about death were also fundamental. The Egyptians believed that, if they lived good lives, they would be reborn and live again in a perfect afterlife. This belief in rebirth underpinned all their myths, rituals, and ceremonies. It profoundly influenced the Egyptians' view of the world.

Right: The Nile River, which flows through Egypt, is the world's longest river. It travels 4,189 miles (6,741 km) northward from East Africa to the Nile Delta, where it flows into the Mediterranean Sea.

The Egyptians worshipped different types of gods: some were gods of the cosmos; some were gods of love, fertility, or wisdom; and others were gods of the underworld or animal gods. Many combined different roles. Gods and goddesses evolved and changed during ancient Egypt's long history, and different gods were worshipped in different regions of the kingdom.

CHANGING MYTHS

Egyptians developed myths to explain the mysteries of the world around them: how the universe was created, why the sun rose and set, how the Nile flooded, and what happened after death.

The myths changed over time, sometimes to make sense of something new. They also varied from place to place. There were different religious or cult centers, each of which had its own chief god or family of gods. The most important cult centers were Memphis, Thebes, Heliopolis, and Hermopolis. As one or another city rose in status, so too their gods and myths became more important and spread. As a result, there are often several different versions of the same myth, and several myths contradict each other.

Until fairly recently, Egyptian myths were not as well known as those from other cultures. Priests and scribes decorated pyramids, temple walls, obelisks, and coffins with gods and stories about them, but no one outside ancient Egypt could read the hieroglyphs. For a long time our knowledge of Egyptian myths came from accounts written in Greek and Roman by historians who visited Egypt, such as Herodotus and Plutarch (c. 46–127 C.E.).

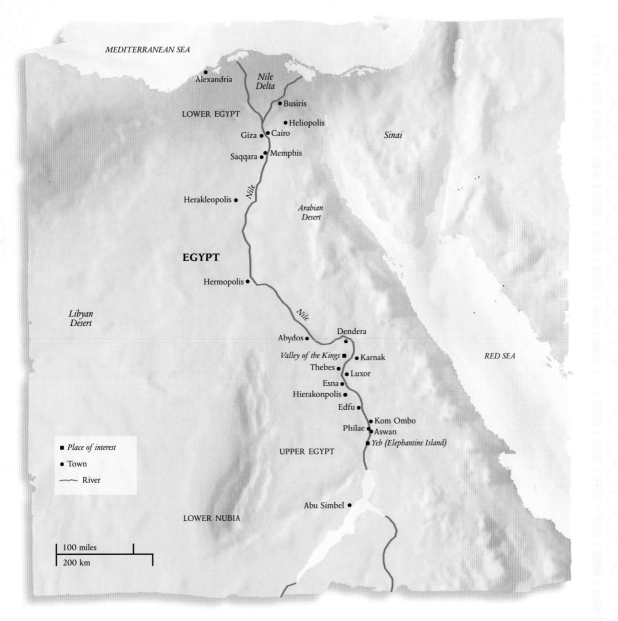

MEDITERRANEAN SEA

Alexandria ·

Nile Delta

· Busiris

LOWER EGYPT

· Heliopolis

Sinai

Giza · · Cairo

Saqqara · · Memphis

Herakleopolis ·

Nile

Arabian Desert

EGYPT

Libyan Desert

Hermopolis ·

Nile

RED SEA

Abydos · Dendera ·

Valley of the Kings ■ · Karnak

Thebes · · Luxor

Esna ·

Hierakonpolis ·

Edfu ·

· Kom Ombo

Philae · · Aswan

■ *Yeb (Elephantine Island)*

UPPER EGYPT

■ *Place of interest*
· Town
River

Abu Simbel ·

LOWER NUBIA

100 miles
200 km

In 1822, a French Egyptologist, Jean-François Champollion, managed to crack the hieroglyph code, which meant historians and archaeologists could finally begin to translate the myths from their original sources. Obviously the sources themselves are fragmented or damaged, and some myths are incomplete. There may still be more to discover, but those myths that we already know reveal a great deal about the real and mythical world of ancient Egypt.

The god Amun, shown with a ram's head, was a
creator god who was worshipped in Thebes
(Luxor). By the time of the New Kingdom
(c. 1550–1069 B.C.E.) he was worshipped
throughout Egypt and had merged with Ra from
Heliopolis to become Amun-Ra.

GODS OF THE COSMOS

Like every other society, the Egyptians wanted to know how the world began, who created the cosmos or universe, and how the sun, humans, plants, animals, and the whole natural world came into being. They looked to their gods for answers and developed myths that explained the mysteries of creation. For the ancient Egyptians, all parts of the universe—the sun, moon, stars, earth, and water—were divine beings. They were gods, and gods had created them.

Each of the main cult centers—Memphis, Thebes, Heliopolis, and Hermopolis—developed its own creation myth and claimed that their chief god was the creator. One of the best-known myths, included in this chapter, comes from Heliopolis. Priests there worshipped the sun god Ra, and believed Atum, a manifestation of Ra, had created the universe. Once the creator god had made the universe and brought order out of chaos, he created other gods. The ones mentioned in this chapter are among the most important Egyptian gods.

How the
World was Made

In the very beginning, nothing existed. There was no night, no day, no land, no sky, no gods or people, no Egypt, world, or universe. There was only darkness and a vast, swirling, bubbling, watery chaos, called Nun, or Nu. But from this chaos a creator god emerged. He was Atum, sun god and creator of all.

Atum was the first and only god. Lying deep in the watery chaos, he thought himself into existence. He emerged from the chaos, shining like the sun, and looked around. "I have no place to stand," he said. So in the place where he first appeared, he created a mound, which emerged out of the chaos as islands appear in the Nile when the floodwaters go down. The mound was the first land.

The god looked around again. There was much to do and he was alone. "Heaven and earth do not exist," he said, "and the things of the earth do not yet exist. I must raise them out of Nun." He decided to make more gods to keep him company and help him create the universe. He spat, sneezed, and vomited. From the mess that came out of his mouth and nose, two beautiful children were created—a son and a daughter.

Atum named his son Shu. He was the god of the air. He named his daughter Tefnut. She was goddess of mist and moisture. Now Atum had brought order to the chaos. He was no longer alone. He and his children lived together on the mound in the middle of the watery sea.

ATUM CREATES HUMANS

Atum watched his children constantly, worrying that something dreadful would happen to them. Once he looked away briefly and, when he turned back, Shu and Tefnut had disappeared. They had wandered away and fallen into the great watery sea. Atum was devastated. He cried until his sight was blurred, searching everywhere for his missing children. Finally, he removed his eye from his face and ordered it to look for his children. Gazing through the darkness, the eye caught sight of the missing children and brought them back to Atum. He was so delighted to see them once more that he wept great tears of joy. His tears fell on the mound and, where they landed, human beings sprang up.

Above: Nut, goddess of the sky, arches over her brother Geb, god of the earth, who is lying on the ground. Their father, Shu, supports Nut and separates them.

SUN AND MOON, EARTH AND SKY

The eye was angry. When it returned to Atum, it discovered that Atum had replaced it with another. To calm the first eye, Atum promised it more power than the second, but this now meant Atum had two eyes. He made the first eye into the eye of the sun and the other into the eye of the moon. He then turned the eye of the sun into a striking cobra to protect him.

Eventually Shu and Tefnut had their own children. They produced twins, a son called Geb and a daughter called Nut (newt). Geb was god of the earth and Nut was goddess of the sky. They were born in a close embrace so Atum ordered their father, Shu, to separate them and keep them apart. Shu did this. He lifted his daughter up high and supported her so that air came between sky and earth. Geb lay down on the ground beneath Nut. From his body appeared plants, green fields, marshes, and the Nile River. When Geb laughed, there were earthquakes, and when he was angry, there was famine in the land. Nut, the beautiful goddess of the sky, remained arched over his body, the tips of her fingers and the ends of her toes just resting on the horizon.

The stars were Nut's children. At night they twinkled from her belly and the light of the moon shone down on the earth. Every morning, Nut gave birth to the sun, which rode across her body in a boat during the daylight hours. At sunset, Nut swallowed the sun. It disappeared from view, traveling inside her body during the hours of darkness until once more Nut gave birth to the sun in the morning.

In this way, Atum and his children created the universe and brought order out of chaos. Later, Geb and Nut produced the next generation of gods.

Right: Ptah was creator and chief god at Memphis. He was depicted in human form, wearing a skullcap and carrying a staff or crook and flail, symbols of kingship.

DIFFERENT CREATION MYTHS

There were many different creation myths and creator gods. In some versions, the mound emerges out of the watery chaos before Atum. In others, Atum is said to have hatched from an egg on the mound or from a lotus flower. Sometimes the primeval water Nun is the first god.

When pharaohs ruled from Memphis, their creator god was supreme. He was Ptah (p-tar) and was believed to have thought the world into being. Other myths feature a creator god called Khnum (k-noom) who was said to have fashioned the whole world and everything in it from clay that he molded on a potter's wheel. Despite variations, all the creation myths have features in common. They all include a first god who creates himself, and describe how he brought order out of chaos, which was critical in ancient Egypt where the natural world could be unpredictable. They also all feature water, which is not surprising given the importance of the Nile River.

Below: Yeb (Elephantine Island) in the middle of the Nile was an important religious center dedicated to the creator god Khnum, who fashioned the universe on a potter's wheel.

DAYS UPON THE YEAR

Atum, or Ra, as he was now known, created the universe and gods. He had two grandchildren, Nut and Geb, who loved each other. Atum had ordered that they should be kept apart but they managed to meet despite him. One day Thoth, god of wisdom, came to Ra with some bad news.

Thoth was a tall, imposing figure with the body and shape of a man, and the head of an ibis. He looked at Ra and said, "Nut, your granddaughter, goddess of the sky, is pregnant."

Ra was furious. He feared that, if Nut produced a son, that son would one day replace him as supreme ruler. He was determined to prevent this from happening.

Right: An antelope and a lion are depicted on a papyrus playing the game senet, c. 1100 B.C.E. Senet was a very popular game. Players moved counters around a board, competing to win a place in the afterlife. Senet boards were painted on tombs so the dead could still enjoy a game.

RA CURSES NUT

Ra summoned Nut into his presence and laid a curse on her. He forbade her to give birth on any day of the year—there were, at that time, 360 days in a year.

Nut was heartbroken and wept bitter tears. She was pregnant but her children could never be born. Her grief was terrible and she did not know where to turn. She went to see Thoth and asked him for help.

Thoth cared deeply for Nut and was moved by her tears, but he knew that no one, not even a god, could break Ra's curse once it had been spoken. However, Thoth was an extremely wise god. There and then he thought of a very clever plan. He told Nut not to lose hope.

THOTH PLAYS A GAME

That evening Thoth went to see his friend Khonsu, god of the moon. Khonsu was a young, handsome god, who loved to play board games. Thoth, who also enjoyed a game, challenged Khonsu to play a game of senet with him.

Khonsu agreed eagerly and suggested that the loser pay a forfeit. Thoth was delighted to accept this arrangement, and the two of them sat down opposite each other and began.

THE EGYPTIAN CALENDAR

The ancient Egyptians were the first to have a 365-day year, although they did not have a leap year as we do. Originally their year consisted of twelve months of thirty days each, making 360 days, but by 2400 B.C.E. they had added five days to bring the year more in line with the solar cycle. The Egyptians called them "the days upon the year" and they were a time of feasting and festivals.

The Egyptian calendar was linked to the movement of the star Sirius, which was at its brightest at the beginning of the year, and corresponded to the annual flooding of the Nile River.

The year was divided into three main seasons, each consisting of four months. The first season, which was known as Akhet, was when the Nile flooded, bringing fertile silt onto the land. The second season, Peret, was when the crops were planted. The third season, Shomu, was when the crops were harvested.

Right: A circular zodiac calendar shows gods, goddesses, and festival days. This calendar dates back to c. 305 B.C.E. and was painted on the ceiling of the Temple of Dendera, on the west bank of the Nile.

Thoth won the first game. "What forfeit must I pay?" asked Khonsu. "A little bit of your moonlight," Thoth replied.

Khonsu smiled as he had plenty of moonlight. They carried on playing, and Thoth won the next game. Once again, Khonsu forfeited a little more light, but he still had plenty and challenged Thoth to yet another game, determined that this time he would win. The friends played all night and Thoth won every game. Finally Khonsu called a halt to the game. He was getting pale and weak and could no longer play. Thoth gathered up all the moonlight he had won and left.

NUT'S CHILDREN ARE BORN

Thoth had been very clever. With all the moonlight he had won, he made five extra days. They did not belong to any year and, because they were outside the year, Nut could give birth to her children on those days without breaking Ra's curse. And this she did. On the first of the five days, Nut gave birth to her eldest son, Osiris. When Osiris was born, there were signs and wonders, and a voice could be heard announcing that a great king had been born who would rule Egypt. In time this happened.

On the second day, Nut gave birth to another child, Horus, later known as Horus the Elder. On the third day, her son Seth was born. God of deserts, Seth came into the world violently. Nut's daughter Isis was born on the fourth day. She was goddess of wisdom and magic, one of the greatest of all goddesses. On the fifth and final day, Nut gave birth to her last child, the goddess Nephthys, devoted sister to Isis.

Ra was very angry at the trick that had been played on him. He was so angry that Nut asked Thoth to look after the baby Osiris for his safety. It was too late for Ra to stop the births but he ordered that the extra five days should be added to the existing year, which would then have 365 days, just as we have today. Thoth's trick affected the moon, too. Ever since Khonsu played senet with Thoth, he has not had enough light to last a whole month. Instead, the moon waxes and wanes every month.

Gods And Goddesses

The Egyptians worshipped a bewildering number of gods. They themselves said there were too many to count. Every village, town, and district had its own gods, and they combined and evolved throughout Egypt's long history.

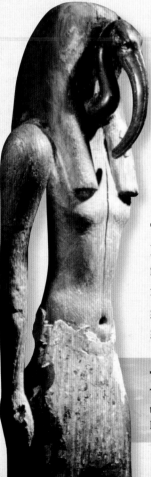

Ra

The sun god was supreme and was worshipped as Ra at Heliopolis. He took many forms, including falcon-headed Ra-Harakhti (far right), wearing a sun on his head, encircled by a cobra. He carried a royal scepter and an ankh, symbol of life.

THE WORLD OF GODS

Evidence indicates that the Egyptians were worshipping sun gods from very early in their history, which is hardly surprising given the importance of sun in their lives. They also worshipped moon and sky gods, fertility gods, and gods of wisdom, truth, and motherhood. Some gods combined several roles in their different aspects, or personalities.

Thoth

Thoth was god of the moon, wisdom, and writing. He could be shown with the head of an ibis, a bird whose beak is like a crescent moon, or as a baboon. Baboons welcome the rising sun, so this symbolized the moon greeting the sun.

Sometimes one god became more important than others. When a cult center, such as Heliopolis or Memphis, rose to importance, so too did its local gods. Some local gods, such as Ra or Atum, became national gods. The Egyptians sometimes then fused them into one, making Atum-Ra, for instance. Historians call this process syncretism, where different practices and beliefs merge. As Egyptians gained new lands, they imported new gods, absorbing them into the pantheon, or world of gods.

Egyptians inscribed images of their gods on temples, tombs, coffins, and papyrus. They also made statues. They incorporated the natural world into their religion, giving the gods animal forms or features. Gods carried symbolic objects or had headdresses to display their status.

Bastet

Cats were regarded as sacred in ancient Egypt. The cat goddess was Bastet, said to be daughter of the sun god and his aggressive nature. There were lively festivals in her honor. Mummified cats have been discovered in tombs.

Isis

Isis was a powerful royal goddess. She was worshipped at Philae but her popularity spread throughout Egypt. She could be depicted as a cow or with cow horns, as a great bird, or as a woman nursing the infant king Horus. She was worshipped as a mother figure, and some historians believe that depictions of her nursing Horus influenced early representations of the Christian Virgin Mary.

DEVASTATION OF HUMANKIND

Before Egypt had human kings, the sun god Ra ruled the land. Harvests were plentiful and the Nile was full of fish. The Egyptians were grateful and worshipped Ra. But he began to grow old. His subjects lost their respect for him and stopped worshipping him.

Ra had aged. He could hear men and women mocking him, saying his bones were like silver, his flesh was like gold, and his hair was the color of lapis lazuli. People disobeyed his laws and wanted to get rid of him. Ra was bitter. He objected to being called old. He wanted to punish humans for their lack of respect but he needed to consult with the other gods first. It had to be done secretly so humans would not know what he was planning.

THE COUNCIL OF GODS

Ra summoned the gods to a special council at his great palace at Heliopolis in the north of Egypt. All the gods—Geb, Shu, Tefnut, Nut, and even Nun—responded to his call. They bowed to the sun god and stood patiently around his throne, waiting for him to speak. Ra told the gods what was happening—that humans were mocking him, calling him decrepit and plotting against him. What should he do? How could he punish them? The gods listened carefully and then Nun spoke. He suggested that Ra should send his daughter Hathor to kill humankind.

Hathor was the eye of Ra. She was a peaceful goddess, but like many of the deities, she had two sides to her character. Ra called her to the council and ordered her to go into Egypt and kill the people for daring to conspire against him.

Opposite: Pillars decorated with the head of Hathor survive today at her temple at Dendera, dating from the first century B.C.E. She was worshipped throughout Egypt as a mother goddess and goddess of fertility.

Immediately, Hathor transformed into her other personality, Sekhmet, the All Powerful. Sekhmet was a ferocious goddess, with the shape and temperament of a great lioness. With a mighty roar, she set off.

Moving swiftly, Sekhmet hunted down humans, seeking them out in the Nile Valley and pursuing them into the desert, where they fled in fear. Wherever she found humans, she killed them, ripping them apart and roaring with pleasure as she slaughtered them. By the end of the day, the land of Egypt ran with blood. Sekhmet was exhausted and returned home to rest before completing her task.

RED BEER

The sun god watched the massacre with growing horror. Ra had wanted humans to be punished but the scale of the killing sickened him. He began to feel pity for men and women. They had learned their lesson. But how could Sekhmet be stopped? Her job was to kill and she was out of control. Once again, Ra spoke with the council. He thought of a brilliant plan but he only had one night to put it into action. When morning came, Sekhmet would start killing again.

Ra sent his swiftest messengers to Yeb island, near Aswan in the south, with orders to collect vast quantities of red ocher, a metallic pigment found only in Aswan. They were to gather as much as possible and bring it back to Heliopolis. Meanwhile, he commanded the kitchen women in his palace to grind millet and corn to make vast quantities of beer. They needed to work fast. When his messengers returned with the red dye, it was added to the beer, turning it a crimson blood red. There was so much liquid, it filled seven thousand huge jars.

By now morning was approaching rapidly. Ra and the other gods took the thousands of jars, full to the brim with red, foaming beer, and made their way to the fields by the Nile. There they spilled the contents out, flooding the fields to a depth of "three palms" (about 9 inches or 22 centimeters). The land was swimming with foaming bloodlike liquid.

They were just in time. Sekhmet had woken up eager to start killing again. She arrived in the fields and saw them drenched with liquid. She roared with pleasure, thinking that the liquid was blood. Eagerly, she lapped up the red beer until she had swallowed every last drop. Within no time, she was completely drunk. Feeling very dizzy, she lay on the ground and fell asleep.

When Sekhmet finally roused herself once more, it was the end of the day. She thought she had killed all the people and returned to Ra's palace. He greeted his fierce daughter warmly, saying, "Come in peace." Instantly, Sekhmet changed back into Hathor. The killing was over and Ra had saved the human race. The people had learned their lesson. From then on, they worshipped Ra as their ruler and god. Every year they also held a festival in Hathor's honor known as the festival of drunkenness.

FOOD AND DRINK

Men, women, and children drank beer with most of their meals. It was made from mashed barley leaves and could be thick and lumpy, so people drank it through wooden siphons to strain the liquid.

Barley and emmer wheat were staple elements of the ancient Egyptian diet. Barley was ground, made into bread dough, and baked in dome-shaped kilns or ovens. The bread was gritty and damaged the teeth, something Egyptologists have discovered from examining mummies.

The Egyptians ate cakes, sweetened with honey or dates, and grew vegetables such as onions, garlic, lentils, leeks, and lettuces. They also cultivated dates, grapes, pomegranates, and other fruits. Wealthier Egyptians ate a wide range of meat, from beef and pork through to wild heron, geese, and even hyena meat. People caught and ate fish from the Nile, including catfish, perch, and mullet.

Right: This painted clay figure of an Egyptian woman grinding corn was made during the Old Kingdom (c. 2686–2181 B.C.E.).

THE SECRET NAME OF RA

Ra had many names. They were inscribed on temples and obelisks throughout Egypt. But he had one name that no one knew. It was the source of all his power and he kept it secret. Isis, goddess of magic, was determined to learn Ra's secret name and become as powerful as he was. She knew he would never tell her willingly.

Even gods grow old, and Ra was now getting very old. He moved slowly, his body trembled, and he often nodded off to sleep when he was sitting on his throne. His head shook and sometimes he dribbled from his mouth.

One day, when Ra was out walking, some dribble fell from his mouth onto the dusty earth, where it made a small muddy patch. Isis was nearby and saw it happen. Quick as a flash, she scooped up the damp piece of earth. Once she was alone, she kneaded and molded the mud into the shape of a snake—the first cobra. She spent a long time at the task, whispering as she worked, breathing magic into the snake until it lived. Once she had brought it to life, she left the snake in the dust by the roadside, where Ra was sure to pass.

A SNAKEBITE

The next day, Ra was again out walking through his land, as he did every day. He passed the snake, which lunged forward and bit him on the ankle, then slithered into the grass and disappeared. Pain from the bite shot through Ra's body and he shrieked in agony. He felt like he was on fire as poison from the bite coursed through his veins.

Ra shivered, broke out into a sweat, and for a while could not speak from the pain. Finally he was able to gasp out words. Who had done this? He had created everything. How could there be anything on earth that was able to hurt him? Was there anyone with magic enough to help him? Hearing his cries, the other gods arrived and stood anxiously around him.

THE IMPORTANCE OF NAMES

Ancient Egyptians believed that a person's name was extremely powerful because it contained the essence of that person, and because without a name, a person did not exist. Naming something gave it life. To know someone's name was to have power over them, and Egyptians believed an enemy could be destroyed if his or her name was written on an object that was then smashed. The myth about Ra's name was written down on a papyrus in around 1200 B.C.E. It is now in the Turin Museum in Italy. A version also survives on a fragment of papyrus in the British Museum, London.

Right: This carved stone stele, or commemorative stone, shows Meretseger (meaning "She who loves silence"), the cobra goddess. She lived in the mountains overlooking Thebes and was worshipped by tomb workers. Pharaohs wore an emblem of a striking cobra, called a uraeus, to frighten their enemies.

Some of the gods wept to see Ra's pain and suffering, but none of them knew what to do. Isis was not only the goddess of magic but also a great healer and was able to bring the dead back to life. Pretending she did not know, she asked Ra to tell her what had happened.

Gasping from pain, Ra told Isis about the snakebite and described his terrible symptoms. He said he was dying. Isis soothed him and said she could cure him but only if he told her his secret name of power, which she could use in a spell. Only that would remove the pain.

Ra knew full well this was a trick, and said, "I am the maker of heaven and earth, I have built the mountains, I am the creator of the waters, I am light and I am darkness, I am the maker of hours and the creator of days, I am Khepri in the morning, Ra at noontime, and Atum in the evening."

Ra hoped that saying these three great names would satisfy Isis. But she listened closely, and heard that he had only spoken the names that everyone knew. He had still not said his secret name.

THE SECRET IS TOLD

The poison continued to cause Ra unbearable agony. Once more Isis urged Ra to tell her his secret name and she would cure him. The pain was so dreadful that finally Ra agreed, but only on certain conditions. He would not speak his name aloud, and Isis was to swear she would never tell anyone except Horus, the son she would have one day. Horus in turn was never to utter the name. Isis agreed. Ra's secret name passed from his heart to the heart of Isis and, with that, Isis used the name to cast a powerful spell that banished the poison.

Isis was now the most powerful goddess of all. She kept her word and told no one until, in time to come, she told Horus. He never told anyone either. To this day no one else knows Ra's secret name of power.

One effect of the spell was to give Ra back some of his youth and health, but he had had enough of ruling. Soon afterward he left the earth and ruled from the skies. His grandson Osiris became ruler in his place.

Opposite: The beautiful temple of Isis was built on the island of Philae, just south of Aswan, during the Ptolemaic period (c. 305–30 B.C.E.), when Egypt was ruled by a dynasty of Greek kings. During the 1960s, a dam was built at Aswan and flooded the temple, which was later moved to the nearby island of Agilika.

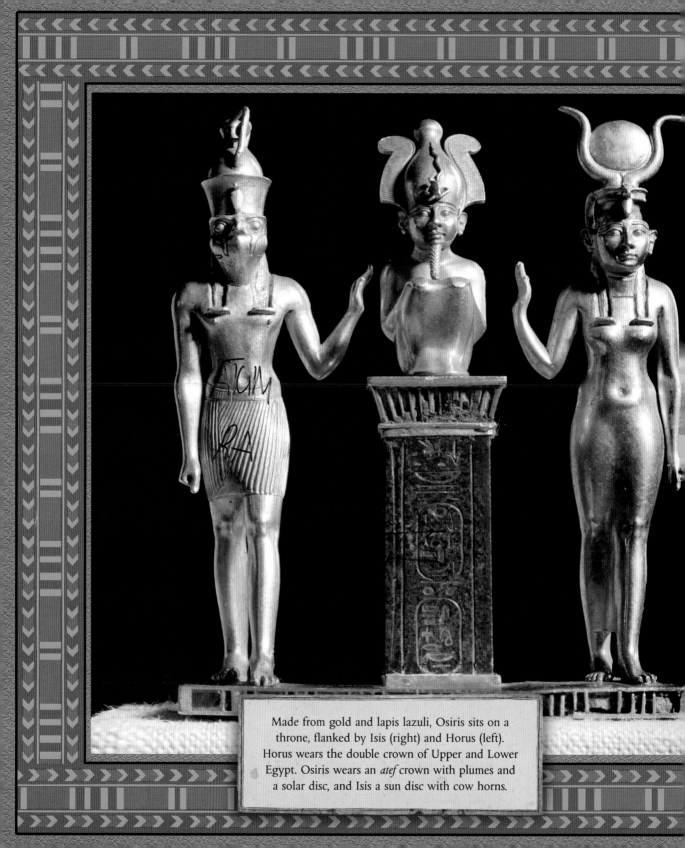

Made from gold and lapis lazuli, Osiris sits on a
throne, flanked by Isis (right) and Horus (left).
Horus wears the double crown of Upper and Lower
Egypt. Osiris wears an *atef* crown with plumes and
a solar disc, and Isis a sun disc with cow horns.

Osiris, Seth, and Isis

The stories of Osiris, his wife and sister Isis, and their brother Seth are some of the best-known Egyptian myths. Seth murders Osiris, king of Egypt. Isis searches for Osiris's body and finally her son, Horus, challenges Seth and avenges his father's death.

The myths survive on papyrus and temple walls, but there was no single continuous version. The ancient Greek historian Plutarch (c. 46–127 C.E.) wrote an account of Osiris's murder. The story of Isis and the Seven Scorpions survives as a spell on a stele that workmen uncovered in 1828. The quarrel between Seth and Horus was recorded on a papyrus from the Twentieth Dynasty. Like all myths, these stories tell us a great deal about the Egyptians' beliefs, especially regarding death and kingship. They stress the importance of a proper burial, provide the origins of mummification, and show how important it was that the right king, chosen by gods, should ascend the throne. They also illustrate that Egyptians believed their gods were just as quarrelsome and indecisive as humans.

THE MURDER OF OSIRIS

After the sun god Ra ascended to the skies, Osiris became ruler of Egypt. He was a kind god and a good and popular ruler. His brother Seth, however, was jealous. He plotted to murder Osiris and take the throne for himself.

Before Osiris became ruler of Egypt, the people were barbarous. They did not obey laws, they fought constantly, ate raw meat, and were even cannibals. Osiris civilized them. With his wife, the goddess Isis, he taught them how to farm and grow crops. The people planted their crops into the black silt left behind by the inundation of the Nile. Farmers scattered seeds by hand, and used oxen and pigs to trample in the seeds. Osiris showed them how to dig ditches to store floodwater, which passed through a network of channels to irrigate the fields. He showed the people which meats were suitable to eat, and how to plant vines and crush grapes to make wine.

Osiris introduced good laws, built temples, and encouraged Egyptians to live peacefully. Under Osiris, Egypt was a prosperous country. The people loved him and called him "the Peaceful One." But there was one person who loathed him: his brother Seth. God of deserts and storms, Seth had been born a violent man. He thought he should be pharaoh and he yearned to have Isis as his consort. His envy was unbearable and he thought constantly of ways to overthrow Osiris.

A BANQUET

Osiris decided to leave Egypt for a while and take civilization to the rest of the world. He left Isis in charge, which annoyed Seth, and set off traveling through distant lands. This gave Seth the opportunity he had been waiting for. First he went to Isis and asked if she wanted his help in ruling Egypt. Isis did not trust the dark and cunning Seth and rejected his offer. So Seth started plotting in earnest. Secretly he met with friends and allies and rounded up a band of seventy-two conspirators who were prepared to help him kill Osiris. All he had to do was wait for Osiris's return.

Above: This tomb painting shows its owner, a skilled tomb worker, Sennedjem, plowing with his wife Iyneferty. In 1886, Italian archaeologists uncovered the tomb, which was at least 3,000 years old. Nothing had been disturbed.

ROYAL MARRIAGES

Gods and goddesses were often said to have married their sisters or brothers. Human kings or pharaohs also married sisters. Because the gods did it, pharaohs may have thought they could do the same and that it emphasized a pharaoh's link to the gods. Brother-sister marriages may also have strengthened a king's claim to the throne. Although it was common for couples to refer to themselves as brother and sister as terms of affection, historians believe that incestuous marriages were not common among the ordinary Egyptian population.

When Osiris returned to Egypt, Seth welcomed him warmly. He invited him to a huge party and banquet at his palace. Osiris was the guest of honor, while all the other guests were Seth's co-conspirators. There had never been such a feast. There were dishes full of exquisite foods, fine wines, and good beer. Court musicians and dancers entertained the guests, and the hours passed pleasantly.

When everyone had had enough to eat and drink, Seth announced that they would play a game. He clapped his hands and servants came into the great hall carrying a beautiful wooden chest. Carved from the most delicate cedar wood and inlaid with ebony and silver, it was a splendid object. Everyone wanted it. Seth then announced the game: whoever could fit into the chest would win it. One by one the guests tried but no one fitted. Either the casket was too small or too long. Finally everyone had tried except Osiris, who, being king, thought the game was a bit demeaning. Seth approached his brother, smiled at him, and asked if he would like to try. Osiris agreed and stepped into the casket. It fitted perfectly, which was hardly surprising because Seth had built it specially for him.

Swiftly Seth and the conspirators crowded around the casket. They slammed down the lid, nailed it shut, and poured molten metal into every crack. Before anyone else found out what had happened, Seth and the conspirators flung the chest into the Nile to destroy all traces of their work. There was no escape for Osiris. Trapped in the casket, with no air to breathe, he suffocated. With Osiris gone, Seth could become ruler of Egypt.

A TAMARISK TREE

The decorated casket carrying the god's body did not sink as Seth had hoped. It drifted northward down the Nile toward the Mediterranean Sea, some say helped by Hapy (happi), the Nile god. It floated into the sea and was carried by the waves to the shores of Lebanon, to the northeast. There it washed up onto a beach near a city called Byblos. The casket with its precious load drifted into the roots of a young tamarisk tree, where it lodged. Over time the tree grew and engulfed the casket, which became part of the tree trunk. The tree grew tall and beautiful, while the strong scent of tamarisk filled the air. Never had such a tree been seen.

The king of Byblos heard about the tree and came to see it. He was struck by its beauty and ordered it to be cut down and brought to his palace. There he had the trunk made into a beautiful pillar for his great hall. No one knew that the pillar, which held up his hall, contained the body of a great god.

Above: Rain falls from the sky goddess Nut onto the mummified body of Osiris, causing plants to grow. Osiris had many roles: he was both a fertility god and lord of the underworld. Little models of Osiris containing millet were put in tombs, where they sprouted, symbolizing rebirth.

THE WANDERINGS OF ISIS

Seth had murdered Osiris and taken the throne of Egypt. Even before being told, Isis knew her beloved husband was dead and that Seth was responsible. Grief-stricken, she cut off her hair as a sign of mourning and was determined to find her husband's body so he could have a proper burial and pass into the afterlife.

Before setting out, Isis took their baby son Horus to the cobra goddess, Wadjet, for safekeeping. She knew he was in danger from Seth. She placed him on an island with Wadjet, then cast the island off into the Nile so Seth could never find them. Then she set off on her quest.

ISIS ARRIVES IN BYBLOS

Isis wandered far and wide, asking everyone if they had seen her husband's body. Eventually some children told her they had seen a decorated chest floating in the Nile. Other children directed her to Byblos.

When Isis arrived in Byblos, disguised as a beautiful woman, she sat down on the seashore, where she met some of the queen's handmaidens, who had come to bathe. Isis fell into conversation with them, but she did not tell them who she was. As they sat, Isis helped the women braid their hair, while breathing an exquisite perfume onto them. When the women returned to the palace, their queen, Astarte (as-tar-tee), asked about the fragrance.

The handmaidens told the queen about the woman they had met, and Astarte invited Isis to come to the palace. She told Isis that her youngest son was gravely ill, and Isis, still in disguise, offered to cure him. She stressed that she must do this in her own way and must not be disturbed.

During the day, Isis cared for the young prince, who—to everyone's amazement—rapidly made a complete recovery. At night, unknown to anyone, Isis turned into a swallow, entered the great hall, and flew around the pillar that contained her husband's body, crying in grief.

ISIS AND THE SEVEN SCORPIONS

Another myth about Isis tells of a time when Thoth warned her to go into hiding with her young son Horus to protect him against Seth. Isis left home with an escort of seven scorpions. She reached a town in the Nile Delta called the Town of Two Sisters. A wealthy woman saw them arrive and slammed her door against them. In revenge, six scorpions passed their poison to the seventh, which slipped under the rich woman's door and stung her young son, almost killing him. The woman was distraught and called for help but no one came, which was perhaps what she deserved.

Isis, who had been given shelter by a poor peasant woman, heard the woman's cries. She could not allow a child to die. Uttering the names of the scorpions in a powerful spell, she cured him. Ashamed of her behavior, the wealthy woman gave her money to Isis and the peasant woman.

Below: Selket was the scorpion goddess. Egypt is home to many scorpions, some of which are very poisonous. The Egyptians believed they could protect themselves against scorpions by reciting Isis's spell and taking a mixture of bread, garlic, and salt.

One night the queen came secretly to the great hall. To her horror, she saw her little son sitting in the middle of a glowing fire. A swallow was flying around the room. Terrified, the queen grabbed her child. But Isis now revealed herself as the great goddess. She told the queen she had been making the young prince immortal but the spell was now broken. The queen and her husband fell to their knees in honor of Isis.

They asked what she wanted. To their surprise, Isis asked for the pillar. She slit it open and there inside was the decorated chest containing Osiris's body. Isis fell on the body, grieving. Then, leaving the pillar, which would forever after be revered as a sacred object, Isis took the chest and set out for Egypt.

Above: Isis and Nephthys mourn the death of Osiris in a tomb painting in the Valley of the Kings, dating from the Nineteenth Dynasty. It was said that their song of grief was used by all Egyptians to mourn the dead.

A FITTING BURIAL

Arriving back in Egypt, Isis hid the chest in the marshes of the Nile Delta and went to find her son. But as luck would have it, Seth was out that night, hunting wild boar on the marshes. He saw the casket glinting in the dark. He threw open the chest, and pulled out Osiris's body, which he hacked brutally into fourteen pieces. He scattered the pieces far and wide, so no one would be able to put the body together again.

Once more the weary Isis set out to find her husband's body and give him a proper burial. With her sister, Nephthys, she traveled on a papyrus boat up and down the Nile, searching for the pieces of her husband's body. Her magic was so great that eventually she found every fragment, except one. Wherever she found a piece of the body, she pretended to bury it and instructed priests to build a shrine and perform the burial rites. For this reason, there are shrines to Osiris all over Egypt.

Eventually Isis assembled all the pieces. Fish had eaten the missing part, so Isis made a replica and attached it to Osiris's body, which was now whole. She and Nephthys transformed themselves into huge birds and hovered over the body, moving their wings gently and singing a song of grief, while the jackal-headed god, Anubis (ah-noo-bis), embalmed the body and wrapped it in fine linen bandages. Gathering up the mummified body, Isis laid it with all the proper rituals in the great temple of Abydos. Isis fanned life into her husband's dead body and he passed over to become lord of the underworld.

Right: Anubis was the god of embalming and cemeteries. Jackals prey on the dead, so Anubis was usually shown as a jackal or a man with the head of a jackal. Some myths said Anubis was the son of Nephthys, who fell pregnant by Osiris after they spent one night together.

The Afterlife

Death features prominently in most Egyptian myths. Egyptians believed in life after death. They thought that after death a person's spirit would be reborn and live on forever in a wonderful afterlife, which they imagined would be like a perfect version of the Nile Valley.

PREPARING THE BODY

Certain things had to happen for a person to enter the afterlife. The body had to be complete and free from decay, and priests had to carry out burial rituals, such as "opening the mouth." It was for these reasons that Egyptians feared dying away from Egypt and why Isis searched so hard for Osiris's body.

Above: Egyptians believed a body had to be preserved for the afterlife. This involved a process called mummification. Embalmers removed a body's vital organs, apart from the heart, and placed them in jars, called canopic jars. They packed salt around the corpse to prevent decay and wrapped it in linen bandages. The body was placed in a mummy case, or sarcophagus, such as the one shown here. Some cases were exquisitely decorated. Food, clothes, jewels, and furniture were put into the tomb for the dead person to use.

Right: A priest wearing the hawk mask of Horus performs the ritual of "opening the mouth" on a pharaoh, whose mummified body stands upright. Egyptians believed this custom, which involved touching a mummy's mouth with ritual instruments, restored living senses to the dead person. The deceased would then be able to eat, drink, talk, and move like a living person.

Below: This wooden model, from c. 2000 B.C.E., shows the type of boat or barge used to carry mummified bodies and mourners along the Nile River for burial. The souls of the dead were believed to travel through the underworld, Duat, on similar boats. The sun god Ra, Isis, and Nephthys accompanied them. There were twelve regions in Duat, one for each hour of the night. Each region held its own dangers.

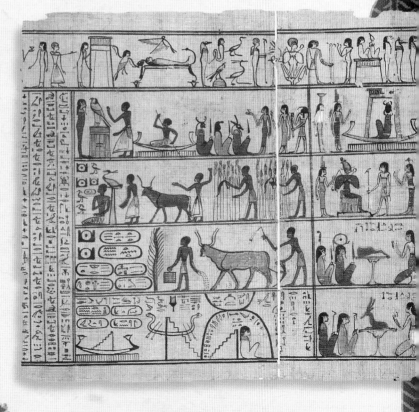

JOURNEY TO THE UNDERWORLD

The dead person's spirit, or *ka*, had to pass through many dangers and trials in a fearful underworld, which the Egyptians called Duat. Finally, the deceased person's heart had to be weighed against its past life to find out if he or she was worthy to pass into the afterlife.

Right: Spells and funerary texts were written on papyrus rolls and put into coffins to help the deceased pass through the underworld into the afterlife. They were often illustrated with brightly colored scenes of the underworld, and it was believed they would provide guidance and protection. Collectively, they are known today as the Book of the Dead.

THE VENGEANCE OF HORUS

Seth was sitting on the throne of Egypt—but Osiris had a son, Horus, who should have been king. When Horus was young, Isis hid him in the marshes, but when he grew up he left the marshes to challenge Seth and claim the throne. Their struggle was long and bitter.

Seth and Horus were summoned to appear before a great council of gods to present their claims to the throne. Horus claimed his right as the son of Osiris. Seth claimed age and strength. Thoth spoke passionately for Horus, and the other gods supported him. Joyfully, Isis told the North Wind to pass the decision to Osiris in the underworld. But Ra, head of the council, was unhappy. He preferred Seth, who was stronger and might cause trouble if he was not chosen.

For eighty years, the gods debated the question without reaching a decision. Finally, they wrote to Neith, an ancient goddess who lived in the Nile Delta, and asked her advice. She said Horus should inherit the throne, warning that if the gods did not do this, the sky would fall and there would be chaos.

The gods agreed, except for Ra, who turned on Horus and accused him of being a weakling. Seth, too, was furious. Was he not a god himself? Did his opinion not count? He refused to accept any decision from a council that included Isis. He threatened to kill a god a day if he was not chosen. Isis cursed him, and the gods began to argue, hurling insults at each other like children.

Ra suggested they move the council to an island in the Nile and try to reach a decision. He gave strict instructions to the ferryman not to let Isis across the water. But Isis turned herself into a frail old woman and bribed the ferryman.

When Isis arrived on the island, the gods were feasting. She disguised herself as a gorgeous young woman. Seth saw her and was overwhelmed by her beauty. She flirted with him and he put his arm around her. Isis told him a sad story: her husband had died, leaving his cattle to her son. But a stranger had stolen her son's

EGYPTIAN LAWS

There may not have been a formalized legal code in ancient Egypt, but many individual laws survive on papyrus. Pharaohs made laws, and harsh punishments were handed out if they were broken. Humans, like the gods, took disputes to law courts, councils, or tribunals. Police, who were paid from the pharaoh's treasury, helped to maintain order and capture criminals. Policemen were armed with staffs and sometimes with dogs or trained monkeys. As today, the police opened investigations following complaints from citizens.

cattle and was trying to turn him out of their home. What should she do?

Not realizing that this was Isis, Seth replied immediately that the cattle and home belonged to her son. This was what Isis wanted.

Shrieking with triumph, Isis transformed into a huge bird, flew to the top of an acacia tree, and screamed that Seth had condemned himself with his own words.

A STRANGE CHALLENGE

Seth was angry, but the gods could do nothing. He himself had admitted that Horus should be king. Seth refused to accept the decision and challenged Horus to a strange contest. They should each change into a hippopotamus and dive underwater. The first to surface would forfeit the throne.

Right: This colossal black granite statue of Horus stands some 10 ft (3 m) tall at the entrance to his temple at Edfu. Shaped like a falcon and wearing the double crown of Egypt, Horus ruled the skies.

43

Opposite: The Temple of Horus lies on the west bank of the Nile, midway between Luxor and Aswan. It took 200 years to build, between c. 237 and 57 B.C.E. According to myth it was the site of the last great fight between Horus and Seth.

Right: Egyptians in papyrus reed boats hunt and spear hippopotamuses. Crocodiles and hippopotamuses were native to the Nile Valley and they were regarded as fearsome creatures.

As the contest got under way, Isis became increasingly fearful that Seth would try to kill Horus. She made a harpoon and hurled it into the water to kill Seth, but it missed and hit Horus, who shrieked in pain. Conjuring the harpoon out of Horus, Isis threw it again and hit Seth. Now he cried in agony, demanding to know why his blood sister should hurt him. Riddled with guilt, Isis removed the harpoon.

The quarrel continued and became increasingly violent. Horus was furious with Isis for helping Seth. He attacked her and fled into the desert. Seth followed and leaped on him, gouging out his eyes. Assuming the throne was now his, Seth returned to the council—but the cow goddess Hathor found and cured Horus. Once more Seth challenged Horus to a contest, this time to a boat race using stone boats.

Horus cheated. He made a ship out of wood painted to look like stone. Seth made his from a rocky mountain peak. When they set sail, Seth sank immediately and Horus won the race, leaving Seth humiliated and enraged. Changing into a fierce hippopotamus, he charged at Horus, overturning his boat. Horus seized a weapon and prepared to fight to the death. But the gods had had enough. Ra ordered them to stop. He sent a message to Osiris for advice.

Osiris replied that Horus, his son, should be king. If the council did not accept his decision, he would send demons to rip out their hearts. Finally Horus became ruler of Egypt. But Ra kept Seth with him as the voice of thunder.

Massive statues of Pharaoh Ramesses II, also known as "Ramesses the Great," and three gods sit in front of the magnificent temple of Abu Simbel. The two temples at Abu Simbel were carved out of rock during the thirteenth century B.C.E.

PHARAOHS AND GODS

Pharaohs ruled Egypt for 3,000 years. Some, such as Ramesses the Great (c. 1279–1213 B.C.E.) or Tutankhamun (c. 1333–1324 B.C.E.), are better known than others. The Egyptians believed their kings were divine beings and were chosen by the gods. When a living pharaoh sat on the throne, the spirit of the hawk god Horus, son of Osiris, was believed to enter his body. For this reason, pharaohs were immensely powerful—it was even considered dangerous to touch them. They were usually men, although women could occasionally hold this office.

Pharaohs were the link between people and the gods. It was a pharaoh's duty to maintain order and to look after the gods so they would continue to help Egypt. According to the myths, gods frequently intervened in the lives of pharaohs. They withheld favors if they were not respected, had a hand in deciding who became ruler, and even fathered royal children.

THE THREE CROWNS

Pharaoh Khufu (2589–2566 B.C.E.), builder of the Great Pyramid of Giza, was rich and powerful. He wanted to know the secret of Thoth's house so he could build himself a funeral tomb worthy of the gods. One day his son Hordedef told him of an ancient magician called Djedi, who could make dead things live again. Khufu was intrigued and told his son to bring the magician to him.

Djedi lived three days' journey from the palace. Hordedef found the magician lying on a mat having his feet massaged. Djedi was 110 years old but he looked like a strong, young man because every day he ate 500 loaves of bread and half a cow, and drank 100 jars of beer. Djedi agreed to go with Hordedef to the palace. When they arrived, the pharaoh rushed out eagerly.

DJEDI PERFORMS MAGIC

Without even greeting the magician, Khufu demanded to know whether it was true that Djedi could bring a beheaded animal back to life. Djedi said he could. Immediately the pharaoh called for a prisoner to be beheaded. Quietly, Djedi refused to undertake the trial, saying it was against the law to murder. Instead he suggested killing an animal.

A goose was brought into the pharaoh's great hall. Djedi cut off the goose's head. He placed the head in one corner of the royal hall, the body in another, and uttered a magic spell. While the pharaoh looked on aghast, the goose's body began waddling toward its head, while the head began to roll toward its body. The two halves of the goose met in the middle of the hall and joined. The goose sprang up as good as new and immediately began to cackle, as geese do. Khufu was astonished. Djedi repeated the trick with a duck and and then with a huge ox.

Now Khufu asked if Djedi knew where the secret Plans of the House of Thoth were hidden so he could use them to design his funeral tomb. Djedi said he knew where they were—in a secret coffer in Heliopolis—but he could not open the chest. Instead,

Djedi prophesied that the oldest son of a woman called Ruddedet would bring the secret to Khufu. Ruddedet was the wife of the high priest of Ra. Djedi said that she was pregnant by the sun god himself and her sons would be pharaohs of Egypt.

Khufu immediately forgot all about Thoth's secret plans. He was much too upset and angry. Did this mean that Ra's sons would usurp his children? Would his sons not be kings? Djedi said the prophecy was true. But he reassured Khufu, saying that his son and grandson would be pharaohs before Ra's sons took over the throne.

Above: The Great Pyramid was built during the reign of Khufu and took about twenty years to complete. It is the oldest and the largest of the pyramids in the necropolis (from the Greek for "city of the dead") at Giza, near modern-day Cairo. Khufu's successors Khafra and Menkaura built pyramids nearby.

BIRTH IN ANCIENT EGYPT

Women in ancient Egypt gave birth while squatting down on two special "birthing bricks." The bricks were believed to determine the future of the child. Babies often died during childbirth so women asked the gods to protect them.

Meshkhent was one of the goddesses associated with childbirth. She was depicted as a birthing brick with a woman's head, or as a woman with a birthing brick on her head. Egyptian women thought Meshkhent would ensure a safe birth, and would announce the baby's destiny when he or she was born. The goddess Heket, who was shaped like a frog, was believed to hasten the last stage of labor. Pregnant women often wore amulets bearing the likenesses of the goddesses to protect them.

Right: Shaped like a hippopotamus with a pregnant belly, Taweret was a fertility goddess who protected pregnant women and mothers. Her ferocious appearance was supposed to frighten evil spirits. This statuette, from c. 620 B.C.E., shows Taweret resting her paws on a hieroglyph, "sa," which means protection.

ROYAL BIRTHS

When the time came for Ruddedet to give birth, Ra sent a group of goddesses to watch over her. Isis and her sister Nephthys led the group, helped by Meshkhent, goddess of birth, and the divine midwife, Heket the frog goddess. Khnum the creator god went with them.

The goddesses assisted at the birth, commanding the first-born to leave the womb. Isis delivered the first child, who was born with a covering of lapis lazuli on his head and gold on his arms and legs. She named him Userkaf, and Meshkhent foretold that he would be king one day. Isis bathed him, and Khnum gave him the gift of health.

Two more sons were born, and the gods repeated their actions. Then the gods departed, leaving the royal children with their human mother, Ruddedet. They left behind a sack, which they hid in a storeroom. Inside the sack were three golden crowns, one for each of the royal children.

Some days later, a serving maid heard sounds of singing coming from the sack. Terrified, she ran to her mistress. Ruddedet opened the sack and saw the three gold crowns. She told her husband, the priest, saying the crowns were favors from Ra but must be kept secret.

The serving maid, who had been beaten by Ruddedet for being lazy, decided to betray her mistress to Khufu. She set out to tell the pharaoh that there were three rivals to his throne—but Ra, who knew everything, sent a crocodile, which seized the maid and dragged her away. In this way, the three crowns remained secret and Ruddedet's children survived to become pharaohs of Egypt.

ROYAL SONS OF RA

Myths such as these could be used to explain or justify political and other changes. Pharaoh Khufu was succeeded by his son Djedefra (2566–2558 B.C.E.), grandsons Khafra and Menkaura, and great-grandson Shepseskaf. Then the Fourth Dynasty, which had been founded by Khufu's father, came to an end—historians are not sure why—and was replaced by the Fifth Dynasty. Userkaf (2498–2491 B.C.E.) was the first pharaoh of the Fifth Dynasty.

LORD OF THE NILE

King Djoser (zoh-ser; 2687–2668 B.C.E.) ruled Egypt during the Third Dynasty. He was a wise and great king who built the first pyramid at Saqqara. It was a wondrous stone tomb, designed by Imhotep, his architect and adviser. But during the eighteenth year of Djoser's reign, disaster struck. The Nile River did not flood.

Usually the Nile rose every year without fail, depositing rich black silt on the land. But this year the Nile was sluggish. Farmers waited, but the rich mud did not come and they could not plant their crops. Fortunately the grain stores were full and Djoser was able to feed his people. But the following year the same thing happened—and for seven years in a row the Nile failed to rise and flood the land.

By the end of these seven years, famine was widespread. Food had run out and plants had shriveled. The strong stole from the weak while the old and sick starved to death. People were desperate. They went to Djoser demanding that he should find the source of the Nile and bring back the floods.

Djoser did not know where the Nile came from. He asked his great vizier Imhotep for advice, saying, "Do you know where the Nile is born? Are there any gods there who can help us?"

Imhotep did not know but he said that he would go to the Temple of Thoth in Hermopolis and see what he could learn. A few days later, he returned and told Djoser what he had found out.

Imhotep told Djoser that the Nile River was born in the south of the land. There was a double cavern on an island—known as Yeb—and from this cavern sprang all the waters of the Nile. The Lord of the Nile was the great god Khnum. Khnum lived on the island and every year, when he was ready, he opened the doors of the cavern to let the waters out. Only Khnum could make the Nile flood again.

DJOSER VISITS KHNUM

Armed with this knowledge, Djoser set off to see the Lord of the Nile. He sailed southward up the Nile in his royal barge until he reached the island of Yeb, birthplace of the Nile. There he found a simple building made of reeds and wood. This was the temple of Khnum. Djoser approached the shrine. He made offerings to the god of bread, cakes, and gold. Suddenly Djoser heard a noise. A majestic figure with human body but the head and horns of a ram was standing in front of him. It was Khnum, Lord of the Nile.

Trembling in fear, Pharaoh Djoser asked what he had done to offend the great lord and why the Nile was no longer flooding Egypt. In reply, Khnum asked why the pharaoh had built himself such a fine and wondrous building as a pyramid but had failed to show respect to him.

Khnum's temple was made of reeds even though the ground around it was rich in precious metals and stones. Why had the Egyptians failed to beautify his temple? Khnum told Djoser that, if he restored to the gods the honor that was their due, then Khnum would restore the Nile.

Right: Imhotep, shown here with a papyrus roll on his lap, was chief architect and adviser to Pharaoh Djoser. A very learned man, Imhotep designed the step pyramid at Saqqara and was also a scientist, astronomer, and doctor. After his death, the ancient Egyptians, and later the Greeks, worshipped him as a god.

53

THE FLOOD RETURNS

Djoser was ashamed and agreed immediately. When he returned to his palace, he ordered Imhotep to build a temple to Khnum that outshone all other temples. And so Imhotep built a magnificent temple. It was filled with gold and silver statues, and its walls were lined with malachite and lapis lazuli. Djoser also commanded great offerings to be made to Khnum. In return, the Nile rose once more and fed the land with rich, fertile silt. From this time on, pharaohs always remembered that it was the Lord of the Nile who gave Egypt its wealth.

PYRAMIDS

Pyramids were stone tombs built to house the dead bodies of pharaohs and their queens. The forerunner of the pyramid was the mastaba, a flat-topped rectangular structure with a shaft leading to a tomb underneath. Mastabas gave way to step pyramids, the first of which was the pyramid of Saqqara, built around 2670 B.C.E. During the reign of Sneferu, in the Fourth Dynasty (c. 2613–2494 B.C.E.),

true pyramids were built, with smooth, sloping sides. They usually formed part of a much larger complex of buildings, often with a causeway leading to the Nile.

Egyptologists believe the pyramid shape may have represented the primeval mound that first appeared from the chaos in the creation myths. Most pyramids contained secret passages and heavy doors, but despite these, they were often ransacked.

Left: The step pyramid of Saqqara as it survives today. It consisted of six stepped layers, representing a gigantic stairway that Djoser could climb to join the sun god in the sky. The pyramid stood 205 ft (62 m) high and was part of a massive complex the size of a small town.

Above: The ancient Egyptians used this device, called a shaduf, to scoop water up from the Nile and pour it into canals for irrigation. The shaduf consisted of a trellis, and a pole with a counterweight on one end and a bucket on the other. Some Egyptian farmers still use it today.

Pharaohs and Gods   55

Temples, Priests, and Pharaohs

The Egyptians built magnificent temples for their gods. The greatest period of temple building was during the New Kingdom (1550–1069 B.C.E.), when a number of fine temples were constructed. They included temples at Luxor, Karnak, Edfu, Dendera, and Philae, and the mortuary temples of western Thebes.

Above: Temple and tomb builders were skilled workers and highly respected. From about 1500 B.C.E., pharaohs chose to be buried in rock-cut tombs in the Valley of the Kings on the west bank of the Nile, across from the city of Thebes (Luxor). The tomb builders lived in this village, Deir el-Medina.

Below: Construction began on the great temple of Karnak, the largest ever built, in the sixteenth century B.C.E. The central temple was dedicated to Amun, then chief god. It included a vast sacred lake, which was used for ritual purification and also symbolized the waters from which life emerged.

TEMPLE CONSTRUCTION

Egyptian temples were not places of worship, like churches and mosques. Ordinary people could not enter beyond their courtyards. Temples were earthly homes for the gods themselves. They were modeled on large houses and reflected the creation myths, often including a sacred lake. Statues of gods and pharaohs stood in front of the temples. The walls were decorated with religious scenes, and hidden in the innermost sanctuary was the deity's shrine.

PRIESTLY DUTIES

Pharaohs were supposed to care for the gods and service their needs, but they appointed priests to carry out the sacred duties. Every so often a god's statue was taken out of the temple and transported along the Nile for a festival. The goddess Hathor, for instance, was taken from Dendera to the temple of Horus every year.

Above: The gateway to a temple was called a pylon. This is the gateway to the Temple of Luxor, built from the fourteenth century B.C.E. On the left is a massive obelisk inscribed with the names of Ramesses II and various gods. In all Egyptian temples, the pylon led to a courtyard, which in turn led to the hypostyle hall. This contained huge columns, often shaped like papyrus plants. The hypostyle hall led into a smaller hall, which opened onto the innermost sanctuary of the god.

Left: Every day, the high priest purified himself and the temple, broke the sealed entrance to the central sanctuary, washed and decorated the statue of the god, and made offerings of food. High priests were powerful people who controlled the temple's wealth and lands.

The great
Queen Hatshepsut

During the Eighteenth Dynasty, Hatshepsut (c. 1479–1458 B.C.E.), daughter of Thutmosis I (thut-mohs-is), declared herself queen and pharaoh of Egypt after the death of her husband Thutmosis II. This was an extraordinary event. It was almost unheard of for a woman to be pharaoh. But this is how it happened.

One day Amun-Ra, lord of the gods, summoned his most important and powerful gods and goddesses to a great council. The goddess Isis; her sister Nephthys; Thoth, god of wisdom; Khonsu, the moon god; Horus and Osiris all came, as did many others. Once they were assembled, Amun-Ra looked at them and announced a golden age was about to begin in Egypt, and that it was in his mind to create a great queen to rule over Egypt and other lands, too. Isis was delighted. In a silvery voice she said that, if Amun-Ra created such a woman, she would grant the queen wisdom.

AMUN-RA FATHERS A QUEEN

Now ibis-headed Thoth spoke up. He said he knew of only one woman who was suitable to carry Amun-Ra's child and be mother to a future queen. Her name was Ahmose Nefertari and she was wife and half-sister to Thutmosis I, then pharaoh of Egypt. She was very beautiful and at that time was on her own in the royal palace at Thebes. Thoth would take Amun-Ra to her.

Amun-Ra disguised himself as Thutmosis I. Thoth cast a spell on the royal palace so that everyone in it fell asleep. Taking Amun-Ra by the hand, Thoth led the great god through the palace, past the guards, and up to the royal bedchamber where Ahmose lay sleeping. Great ebony doors led into the chamber. Amun-Ra passed through the doors, which closed behind him, and found Ahmose sleeping on a lion-shaped couch. He sat next to the sleeping woman and held her face, breathing his spirit into her nostrils.

Above: The dramatic mortuary temple of Queen Hatshepsut is at Deir al-Bahri, near Thebes. Hatshepsut ruled Egypt for about twenty years during the Eighteenth Dynasty. She took on all the trappings of a pharaoh and is sometimes shown with a pharaoh's beard. Egypt flourished under her rule.

As Amun-Ra did so, Ahmose dreamed that she was bathed in light and heard a voice that said, "Rejoice, most fortunate of women, for you shall bear a daughter who shall be the child of Amun-Ra, who shall reign over the Two Lands of Egypt and be sovereign of the whole world."

KHNUM FASHIONS THE ROYAL DAUGHTER

Next Amun-Ra went to Khnum, the creator god, who fashioned humans on his potter's wheel. He instructed Khnum to create a daughter, who would be queen. The god molded two identical figures: one was the future Hatshepsut and the other was her *ka*, or spirit. Standing beside him as he worked was Heket, the frog-headed goddess. Her job was to breathe life into the figures.

As Khnum worked, he spoke to the girl he was creating, saying, "I am forming you of the substance of Amun, god of Karnak. I give you the lands of Egypt and her people, and I will have you appear in glory as king in the role of Horus. You will be supreme among men, as has been commanded by your father."

When it was time for Ahmose to give birth, Khnum and Heket led the pregnant queen to the birthing chamber. They told the queen that her child would be greater than any king born before her. In the birthing room, Meshkhent, goddess of birth, was waiting to protect her. With her was the god Bes. He was a dwarflike figure with pointed ears, a flat

Left: This relief from a wall in Hatshepsut's mortuary temple shows her kneeling between Amun and his standing consort Amunet. It was very rare for a woman to be a pharaoh, but Hatshepsut claimed divine birth. Scenes from the myth of her divine conception and birth decorate the temple.

WOMEN IN ANCIENT EGYPT

By and large, women in ancient Egypt had greater status and independence than other women in the ancient world. They could own property, sign legal documents, and earn the same amount as men. Women were seen as equal to men and were treated with respect. Society did, however, give women and men different roles and different work.

Women's daily lives varied depending on their social status. A woman's main role was to be a wife and mother. She managed the household and could also work outside the home. Middle-class women could be midwives, ladies-in-waiting, temple administrators, or priestesses. Lower-class women worked in the fields or as brewers, bakers, perfume makers, or servants. Elite women could become queens, but usually just as the wives of pharaohs. However, although it was very rare—and normally only occurred after the death of a male relative—Hatshepsut is not believed to have been the first queen to take power over ancient Egypt. The earliest may have been Meryt-Neith, in the 3rd millennium B.C.E.

Right: A detail from a tomb painting dating from c. 1425 B.C.E. shows female musicians playing the harp and lute. Women often worked as court musicians or dancers. The tomb is that of Rekhmire, a high-ranking royal official.

face, bowed legs, and feathers on his head. Bes was jolly but grotesque, and his appearance frightened away evil spirits, which is why he too protected new mothers and babies.

With a goddess kneeling in front of her to deliver the baby, and Meshkhent standing behind her, Ahmose had an easy birth. The queen presented her baby daughter to Amun-Ra, who displayed his daughter to the assembled gods. He blessed the new baby Hatshepsut and gave her the kiss of power so that she would become queen, which in due course she did.

THE PRINCE AND THE SPHINX

There was once a prince called Thutmosis. He was the son of Pharaoh Amenhotep II (1427–1401 B.C.E.) and grandson of Thutmosis III, who succeeded Queen Hatshepsut. One day he had a strange vision.

Thutmosis was Amenhotep's favorite son but he had many brothers and half-brothers, who were jealous and plotted against him. They tried to turn their father against Thutmosis and to humiliate him. They spread cruel rumors about Thutmosis suggesting that he did not honor the gods, and even plotted to kill him.

THUTMOSIS GOES HUNTING

Thutmosis always honored the gods, who smiled on him. His father continued to love him greatly, despite his brothers' whisperings. But the troubles with his brothers distressed Thutmosis and he spent less and less time in the royal palace at Memphis. He was an avid huntsman and skilled charioteer and horseman. He went on hunting expeditions to Upper Egypt, chasing after gazelle, antelope, and wild lions for mile after mile, eventually bringing them down with skillfully placed arrows. He also sought solitude in the mountains.

One day there was a great festival at Heliopolis for the sun god Ra. Being a prince, Thutmosis had to attend—but at the earliest opportunity he left the ceremonies to go and hunt on the edge of the desert. He also wanted to see the great pyramids.

Thutmosis left at dawn in order to travel as far as possible before the searing heat of the day. He set off with two trusted servants and drove his own chariot past Saqqara and its great step pyramid, onward into the vast stretches of the Libyan Desert.

Once in the desert, Thutmosis coursed after gazelles, but the sun grew too hot for hunting. The prince and his servants stopped to rest in the shade of some palm trees not far from the great pyramids of Giza. Thutmosis wanted to be on his own and to pray to the sun god Harmachis, so, telling his servants to wait, he drove his chariot further into

Left: This wall painting from an Eighteenth Dynasty tomb shows Nakht, a royal astronomer and scribe, hunting birds in the Nile marshes. This was a common pastime for wealthier people. Cats were used to flush out the birds, which were killed by throwing sticks at them.

the desert. As he approached Giza, the midday sun glinted down on the pyramids, turning their tips to gold. Nowhere else in the world could equal such splendor.

THUTMOSIS HAS A VISION

As Thutmosis gazed at the pyramids, he became aware of a vast object rising out of the sand. It looked like the head and neck of a huge animal. As he drew nearer, he saw it was a massive carving of a sphinx. Over the centuries, sand had blown against the mighty creature until it had been almost entirely buried.

Thutmosis approached the Sphinx. He had heard of this wonder and knew it represented the god Harmachis, but he had never seen it before. He gazed at the creature's majestic face. On its head it wore the royal headdress decorated with symbols of power: the uraeus cobra and the *wadjet*, eye of the sun god.

As Thutmosis contemplated the Sphinx, he prayed to Harmachis to end his problems. When he finished, he heard a great rumbling and the sand shook. He looked up and saw the Sphinx had moved. It looked like a massive cat, trying to struggle out of the sand.

The Sphinx peered down at Thutmosis and spoke in a powerful but kindly voice, saying, "I am Harmachis, your father, and father of all pharaohs of the Upper and Lower Lands. Listen to me and I will give you my kingdom on earth. You shall wear the White Crown and the Red Crown. You shall rule the Two Lands from one end to the other. All this will happen if you protect me. See how the sand has closed in around me. It smothers me, and it hides me from my people. If you are a good son, clear away that which holds me down so that the people may once again come to me and worship."

When the Sphinx stopped speaking, sunlight seemed to shine out from it, dazzling Thutmosis, who fell to the ground insensible. When he recovered, the sun was sinking and the Sphinx was still. Thutmosis remembered his vision. Or could it all have been a dream? Either way, he swore to the gods that he would do as he had been asked.

Thutmosis found his servants, who had been searching anxiously for him, and they returned to Memphis. Immediately Thutmosis ordered workmen to restore the Sphinx and clear away the sand. From that day onward, everything went well for Thutmosis. Amenhotep named him successor, and eventually he became Pharaoh Thutmosis IV.

THE MYSTERIOUS SPHINX

Few images, apart from the pyramids, symbolize ancient Egypt more than the Sphinx. It is a mysterious creature, and many people confuse it with the sphinx of ancient Greece. In a Greek myth, the sphinx was a cruel winged creature—part lion, part woman—who challenged travelers with a riddle, killing them if they did not answer correctly. The ancient Egyptian sphinx was a benevolent guardian. It had a lion's body and a man's head, usually that of a pharaoh, and was linked to the sun god. The Egyptians called sphinxes *shesep-ankh* ("living statues"), but we use the Greek word "sphinx." They appeared on jewelry, and statues of sphinxes lined the avenues in temples, such as Karnak. The Great Sphinx of Giza is the most famous. It represents Harmachis, or Horus of the Horizon, the sun god rising in the east.

Lying between the paws of the Great Sphinx is a stone slab known as the Dream Stele. Thutmosis IV ordered the building of the stele, which tells the story of his dream. He did restore the sphinx, but Egyptologists believe he made up the story of his dream to legitimize his right to be king because his father did not name him as his successor.

Opposite: The Great Sphinx at Giza is pictured with the pyramid of Khafra in the background. Measuring 240 ft (73 m) long and 65 ft (20 m) high, the Sphinx is more than 4,500 years old. It was carved out of a natural limestone outcrop for Pharaoh Khafra (2558–2532 B.C.E.) and may have his face.

THE DOOMED PRINCE

In the past there was a pharaoh who was rich and happily married but had no children. Every day he prayed to Ra for a son. Eventually the gods agreed to his request and a son was born. But the seven Hathors, the goddesses of fate, visited the baby and pronounced an awful destiny: the prince would die from the bite of a crocodile, a snake, or a dog.

The pharaoh was determined to save his son. He ordered a stone house to be built, filled it with servants and luxuries, and gave orders that his son should never be allowed out. His son grew into a strong boy but he was lonely. One day he spied a man passing with a dog. He asked one of his servants what it was. The servant told him, and the prince demanded a dog for himself. Reluctantly his father let him have a small puppy. The prince and his dog, a greyhound, became devoted companions.

Eventually the boy became a handsome young man. He was restless and asked his father why he was shut away. His father told him about his doom. The young prince said he was not prepared to shut himself away. He would go into the world and meet his doom if that was the will of the gods. Armed with weapons, the young prince set out, with his faithful greyhound following.

A SYRIAN PRINCESS

The prince traveled through Egypt, Sinai, and Palestine until he finally reached a place called Naharain in Syria. He made his way to the capital city, which was humming with excitement. The king of Naharain had a beautiful daughter who was locked away in a tall tower on the summit of a cliff. The king had promised that the first prince to scale the tower could marry his daughter.

All the Syrian princes were eager to try, but none had yet succeeded. When the young Egyptian prince arrived, the Syrian princes greeted him warmly. They asked who he was. He told them he was the son of an Egyptian charioteer but his mother had died and his

Above: The double temple of Kom Ombo, shown here, was dedicated to two gods: the crocodile god, Sobek, and the falcon god Haroeris (Horus the Elder). The temple contains mummified crocodiles.

father had remarried, so he had left home. He asked what the princes were doing, and they told him about the king's daughter.

Over the following days, the prince watched while one prince after another tried and failed to climb the tower. Eventually he decided to try. It was a steep and difficult climb but he succeeded and arrived at the princess's chamber. The king heard of his success and was horrified at the thought of a commoner marrying his daughter. He sent men to kill the prince, but the princess clung to him saying she would kill herself if she could not marry him. The king relented and the prince and princess were married.

PLANTS AND ANIMALS

Ancient Egypt was home to many different animals and plants, which the Egyptians incorporated into their myths and beliefs. Lions, gazelles, antelopes, and hyenas roamed the deserts and appear in many myths. There were crocodiles and hippopotamuses in the Nile. The Egyptians hunted them but also worshipped them as gods. It was believed that, if priests made offerings to the animal gods, perhaps they would not attack people.

Plants also had sacred meanings. The papyrus had practical uses but was also believed to have grown on the original mound of land spoken of in the creation myth and was the symbol for Lower Egypt. Many gods are shown holding a papyrus reed, which was also used to decorate temples. The lotus, or blue water lily, symbolized Upper Egypt. Because its flower closed at night and reopened in the day, the Egyptians believed it was linked to the sun god, who disappears at night and is then reborn at dawn.

Right: This bracelet depicts Khepri, god of the morning sun, as a scarab or beetle. The Egyptians believed he rolled the sun across the sky, as a beetle rolls its young in a ball of dung.

Below: This statue of the crocodile god Sobek dates from the sixth century B.C.E. Worship of Sobek began as an attempt to pacify crocodiles, but the god also came to symbolize the produce of the Nile.

ESCAPING THE FIRST DOOM

Now that they were married, the prince told his new wife who he was and all about his prophesied doom. Hearing this, the princess urged him to kill his dog, but the prince refused, saying it would never harm him. The princess was worried but decided she would always be there to look after her husband.

The prince and princess traveled back to Egypt to his home. Unknown to the prince, there was a crocodile in the river, waiting for him. Fortunately a huge giant of a man also lived in the prince's town and watched over him. The giant warned the prince not to leave his house at night and every night bewitched the crocodile so that it could not move.

One day the prince held a great feast in his house. Afterward he fell fast asleep. His wife stayed up, washing and anointing her body. She heard a rustling sound and saw a great snake sliding across the floor toward her husband. Quick as a flash she filled a bowl with milk and honey and placed it on the floor. The snake drank the milk and became drowsy. The princess seized a dagger and sliced the head off the snake. Then she woke the prince and told him she had saved him from one of his dooms: perhaps the gods would help her overcome the others.

THE PRINCE FALLS IN THE RIVER

A few days later, the prince was walking near the river with his dog. The dog took off after some wild fowl and the prince followed, running behind. Moving too fast, the dog fell into the river and the prince fell in after him. The waiting crocodile grabbed him and closed his jaws around the prince's body. As he did so, the crocodile said, "Behold, I am your doom, following after you…"

UNFINISHED DOOM

The story of the Doomed Prince is incomplete. The papyrus on which it was written is badly damaged so we will never know what finally happened to the prince.

Modern versions all end with the prince dying. One version says the prince escaped the crocodile but was killed by robbers because his dog unwittingly led him into danger.

This drawing of a cat guarding six geese and a nest of eggs is dated c. 1120 B.C.E. and comes from an ancient Egyptian fable. Fables were often used to criticize society. This image may suggest that a servant bides his time before turning on his master—as the cat waits till the chicks are hatched before eating his fill.

MAGICAL STORIES AND LEGENDS

As well as the myths of the gods, tales of magic, fantasy, and extraordinary adventures have survived on papyrus and tombs. Some of the stories in this chapter probably originated with storytellers and were told for entertainment in villages throughout ancient Egypt before scribes wrote them down. The tales included here were written down between c. 1800 and 1200 B.C.E.

Magic and mystery played an important role in the everyday life of most Egyptians, and stories about magicians and tricksters and their extraordinary skills probably provided an exciting escape from the difficulties of everyday life. The gods were said to work great magic, but so, too, were certain legendary individuals, such as Se-Osiris, who was said to be the greatest magician in Egypt. Egyptians had a strong sense of right and wrong, and the stories include moral lessons, just like most fables.

The Enchanted Island

One day a ship docked at the island of Yeb on the Nile River. On the ship was a royal official who had been on a trading mission to Nubia, but his ship had been lost in a storm and he was forced to return to Egypt on this vessel. He was terrified of telling the pharaoh about his failure, fearing the pharaoh would have him executed.

While the official huddled in his cabin, the ship's captain came in. He asked what the problem was, and the official explained. The captain tried to reassure him, saying disasters sometimes ended well. To cheer the official up, he would tell him a story from his own life.

The captain told the official that many years previously he had sailed on a fine boat with a crew of 120 sailors. Disaster struck when a violent storm suddenly appeared while they were sailing in the middle of the Red Sea. The storm was the worst he had ever seen. The wind howled, rain lashed down, and enormous waves, the size of mountains, crashed down onto the boat, which eventually sank. Everyone aboard was drowned except for the sailor. He was washed onto an island, where he lay exhausted for three days and nights.

On the fourth day, the sailor woke up hungry and thirsty and set out to explore the island. It was lush and green. There were figs, grapes, berries, melons, cucumbers, and wildfowl on the island, and its sparkling pools were full of fish. The sailor ate his fill, then lit a fire and gave thanks to the gods for saving his life.

As the smoke rose from the fire, the shipwrecked sailor saw the trees shivering violently, and the ground beneath him began to shudder. He heard a hissing sound and, when he looked up, he saw a giant snake, more than 100 ft (30 m) long, coming toward him.

The creature had golden scales, eyebrows of lapis lazuli, and wore a pharaoh's beard. The sailor was rooted to the spot in terror, expecting the snake to strike. To his surprise, it began to speak.

Above: Sailing barges such as this one, seen in an Eighteenth Dynasty wall painting, carried goods from Nubia. Nubia was a kingdom south of Egypt. Eventually the Egyptians conquered Nubia, so obtaining its mineral wealth of gold and amethyst, and goods such as ivory, ebony, and animal skins that came from further south in Africa.

Rearing up to a great height, the snake demanded to know what the sailor was doing on his island. If the sailor did not tell the truth, the snake said he would burn him alive. At first the sailor was struck dumb, but after a few moments he was able to compose himself and form words. The sailor explained exactly what had happened.

Now the snake spoke more gently. He told the sailor not to be miserable. The snake explained that, if the sailor had been shipwrecked on the island, it was because the gods wanted it to happen. There was no need to be worried. In four months' time his friends would sail by and take him back to Egypt. In the meantime, he and the sailor would live as friends.

Magical Stories and Legends 73

THE LAND OF PUNT

To the Egyptians, Punt was an exotic place. Historians are not certain where Punt was but think it was probably in eastern Africa, near what is now the Sudanese coast. Our only information comes from Egyptian records. Pharaoh Sahure in the Fifth Dynasty organized the first known expedition to Punt, and later Queen Hatshepsut sent five ships there on a trading mission to buy frankincense and myrrh.

Egypt was very wealthy. It traded with Nubia and Punt in the south, Canaan in the east, and Libya to the west. Later, Egypt traded with Greece and the Babylonian Empire.

The Egyptians exported farming produce, linen, papyrus, and manufactured goods. They imported slaves, gold, silver, ivory tusks, incense, perfumes, and oils as well as animals such as horses, baboons, and lions.

A TALE WITHIN A TALE

The serpent told the sailor that he too had a story but it was very sad. Many years ago, he said, he had lived on the island with his wife and daughter and his brothers and their wives and children. There had been seventy-five of them altogether. But one day a shooting star hit the island and all the snakes were killed, except for him. For a long time the snake had wanted to die, but eventually he learned to accept the will of the gods.

Hearing this, the sailor said that when he returned to Egypt he would tell the pharaoh of the snake's goodness and arrange for myrrh, incense, perfumes, and other precious offerings to be sent to the snake.

The snake laughed. He told the sailor to look around him. The island had everything the snake could want. And anyway, he was the Prince of Punt, the land where Egypt got all its incense. There was nothing the sailor could give him. Once the sailor had gone, his enchanted island would sink back into the sea and never be found again.

Everything happened just as the snake said it would. For four months, the sailor lived happily on the enchanted island, until one day he saw a ship approaching. Looking out from a tall tree, he could see that it was an Egyptian ship. This was the ship that would take him home. The sailor said farewell to the snake, bowing low with respect. The snake blessed the sailor and wished him a safe return to his home. He gave him precious gifts: perfumes, oils, eye paint, ivory, incense, and many other fine goods. The sailor set off and, when he looked back, the island had completely disappeared.

Two months later, the sailor arrived in Egypt. He went to see the pharaoh and gave him all the precious goods that the snake had given him. In return, the pharaoh made the sailor an official of the court.

When the captain finished his story, he looked encouragingly at the official, saying that this was proof that disasters ended well.

But the official was not comforted. "Who gives water to a goose on the day it is to be killed?" he asked, and went off fearfully to see the pharaoh.

Opposite: Temple reliefs at Deir el-Bahri record scenes from a famous expedition to Punt that Queen Hatshepsut organized in the fifteenth century B.C.E. Two servants load boats with exotic goods.

THE CLEVER THIEF

Ramesses III (c. 1183–1152 B.C.E.) was fabulously rich. He worried constantly that robbers would steal his wealth. Even royal tombs were not safe from thieves, despite all their secret passages and sealed doors. One day he summoned his architect and told him to build a treasure house that no thief would ever be able to break into.

Ramesses trusted his architect completely, and his architect used only the most trusted and skilled workers. The new treasure house consisted of a single room made of solid stone. It had no windows and only one door. Ramesses checked the building and was satisfied. He filled the room with all his treasure: golden statues, perfume, sparkling gemstones, decorated furniture, and jewelry of all kinds. The room was packed from floor to ceiling with his wealth. The door was closed and sealed with his royal seal, and guards were posted outside. No one could enter.

MISSING TREASURE

Time passed and, although there were other robberies in the area, the pharaoh's treasure remained untouched. After some years the pharaoh's architect died—and then strange things started to happen. One day Ramesses was walking past his treasure house. He decided to break the seal and have a look at his treasure. When he entered the room, he felt something was wrong. He had so much treasure he could not tell if anything was missing, but it felt as if someone had been there. The guards insisted that no one had passed them—and, anyway, the seal had not been broken. So the pharaoh resealed the room and went away.

A week later, Ramesses broke the seal and went into his strong room again. This time there was no mistake. Some treasure was definitely missing. The pharaoh ordered metal traps to be set in the room to catch the thief, doubled the guards, and resealed the door.

When the pharaoh entered the room the next morning he was met by an extraordinary sight: a man had been caught in one of the metal traps. He was dead, naked, and had no head. How had it happened? What did it mean? The door had been sealed, there were no windows, and no one had passed the guards.

The pharaoh was furious. He ordered the dead man's headless body to be displayed high on the palace walls. It was a dreadful but crafty thing to do. Without a proper burial, there could be no afterlife, and the pharaoh hoped the thief's accomplice or family would be so distressed that they would reveal themselves. But this did not happen.

The next morning the body had disappeared! When the pharaoh demanded to know how this had happened, his terrified guards told him that a wine merchant had tricked them into drinking too much wine. They had passed out and when they woke the body had gone. The pharaoh realized that the wine merchant must have been one of the thieves. He was beside himself with rage, but had a sneaking admiration for such a clever man. The guards, of course, were punished dreadfully.

Right: This gold bracelet decorated with a lapis lazuli scarab comes from the tomb of Shoshenq II, a pharaoh of the Twenty-Second Dynasty. His was the only tomb from that dynasty that was not plundered.

LAYING A TRAP

Now the pharaoh came up with a plan of his own. He promised his daughter's hand in marriage to anyone who told her the cleverest secret of all, no matter how wicked. He felt that such a clever thief would want to boast. And he was right. That night the thief, muffled in a robe, came to the pharaoh's daughter.

Below: Many jewels were believed to protect their wearers. This gold collar is designed in the shape of the vulture goddess, Nekhbet, who protected mothers and children.

Looking furtively around, the thief confessed that his father had been the royal architect. When his father built the treasure house, he made a secret entrance from two interlocking stone bricks. When they were slid apart, it was possible to enter the room.

After his father's death, the thief and his brother started robbing the treasure house. But his brother had been caught in the pharaoh's man trap. In terrible pain and unable to escape, he told the thief to cut off his head and take it away so no one could identify him. The thief did this, but the next day he tricked the guards and stole the body from the palace walls so his brother would have a proper burial.

When he had finished his story, the thief turned to the pharaoh's daughter and asked whether this was not the cleverest secret she had ever heard. She said it was and offered to let him kiss her hand. An arm came out of the robe to take her hand. The princess held it tight and called loudly for the guards to capture the thief. But then she screamed in horror: the hand she held was cold and dead—the thief had disappeared, leaving a corpse's hand in hers. Once more the clever thief had fooled the pharaoh.

Ramesses was so impressed by the thief's cunning that he offered a reward and pardon if the thief gave himself up. Some say that the thief married the pharaoh's daughter and was made a court minister, but it is unlikely.

JEWELRY

The Egyptians produced stunning jewelry. The country was rich in gold, which was extracted from mines in the south. Goldsmiths beat or molded the metal into beautiful bracelets, necklaces, rings, and protective amulets. The desert was rich in semiprecious stones such as amethyst and carnelian, which were added to gold to make ornaments. Turquoise from the Sinai region and lapis lazuli from Afghanistan were also used. Jewels and treasure were buried with pharaohs and high officials for use in the afterlife, but although tombs were carefully constructed, tomb robberies were common. Severe punishments were given to anyone found guilty of robbing a tomb, but despite this some thieves even hacked gold death masks off the dead bodies of pharaohs.

THE LAND OF THE DEAD

A prince called Setna lived in Thebes with his son, who was called Se-Osiris. Although Se-Osiris was young, he was already a wonderful magician and wise beyond his years. He even took his father to visit the Land of the Dead.

One day Setna and his son were watching two funeral processions going along the street. The first was for a rich man. Servants pulled a sledge on top of which was a beautiful mummy case inlaid with gold. Inside was the dead man's body, wrapped in fine linen. Priests and family chanted to the gods and carried luxurious goods that the dead man would need in the afterlife: food, linen clothes, gold, turquoise, and other precious things. They would take him down the Nile to a splendid tomb.

The second procession was very different. It was for a poor man. His two sons carried their father's body, wrapped in a mat, in a simple wooden case. They crossed the river to bury their father in a desert pit.

SETNA ENVIES THE RICH MAN

Setna sighed. Even in death, it was better to be rich, he said. But Se-Osiris disagreed. To his father's great surprise, he said, "I pray the poor man's fate may be yours and not that of the rich man."

Setna asked his son how he could say that. Se-Osiris offered to show him but it would mean going to the Land of the Dead, which was extremely dangerous. If they were not careful, they might not return.

Setna trusted his son and agreed. Se-Osiris took his father's hand and uttered powerful words. Immediately, the *ba* spirits of Setna and Se-Osiris left their bodies in the form of two huge birds. As the sun sank over the horizon, the two birds spread their wings and flew westward to Duat, the Land of the Dead. They arrived in time to see Ra passing into Duat on his nightly journey through the underworld. He was sitting in a great boat that was decorated with lapis lazuli, turquoise, and amethyst.

Above: Many New Kingdom pharaohs were buried in the Valley of the Kings on the west bank of the Nile. The Egyptians believed the afterlife was in the west where the sun set. People lived on the east bank and crossed the Nile to bury their dead in the west.

With Ra were the *ka* spirits of everyone who had died that day. While Setna looked on, gods hauled on golden ropes to pull Ra's boat along the River of Death that flows through the underworld.

Slowly, the boat passed through one region after another, until it reached the huge wooden doors that opened onto the judgment hall of Osiris. The doors opened, turning on great pivots—and Setna heard a fearful shriek of pain. Looking down, he saw that one of the pivots was resting on the right eye of a man who was lying on the ground. Whenever the doors opened, the pivot turned agonizingly in his eye socket.

The *kas* of the dead climbed out and the boat continued on its way. The judgment hall was a fearsome place. The ceiling was a mass of flames, and the walls were made of writhing serpents. Osiris sat on a throne, wrapped in his mummy bandages and carrying his royal scepter. Next to him were forty-two judges. The goddesses Isis and Nephthys stood behind Osiris. A huge set of weighing scales was set in front of his throne.

WEIGHING THE HEART

Jackal-headed Anubis was also present. It was his job to weigh the hearts of the dead to find out whether their owners had lived good or bad lives. He placed

Above: A scene from the Book of the Dead shows Anubis weighing the hearts of the dead. Ammut, devourer of hearts—part lion, part crocodile, and part hippopotamus—sits below the scales. The judges represent the forty-two districts or nomes of Egypt. Osiris sits on the throne.

A PERSON'S SPIRIT

Egyptians believed a person's spirit consisted of three main elements: *ka*, *ba*, and *akh*. The *ka* was a person's soul or vital force. It was created at birth and was a perfect double. It needed the body to continue living after death, which is why bodies had to be preserved. The *ba* was a person's personality: it was what made someone who they were. The Egyptians thought the *ba* looked like a bird with a human head. The *akh* was a person's immortality. Other important elements of a person were their name and their shadow.

an ostrich feather in one of the weighing scale's dishes. Then he took the heart from the first *ka*. Its owner had been an evil man. As Anubis moved the heart toward the scales, the *ka* cried, "Oh my heart. Do not testify against me. I am pure. I have not done evil."

But these words did no good. Anubis placed the heart on the scales. It was heavy with evil deeds and sank lower and lower. Ammut, the fearsome god who devoured hearts, put the heart into his mouth and ground it between his teeth. The spirit of the heart's owner was cast into the everlasting pits of fire.

Now Anubis took the heart that belonged to the poor man whose funeral Setna and Se-Osiris had seen earlier. Anubis placed the heart on the scales, but this time the heart was so free of sin that the scale soared upward.

All the judges cried out that this heart belonged to a man who had truly lived a good life. Osiris welcomed the man's spirit and said he should go into the Fields of Peace and live in plenty forever.

SETNA LEARNS THE LESSON

Setna had watched all these things in wonder. But what had happened to the rich man? Se-Osiris told him that the man shrieking in pain with the pivot turning in his right eye had been the rich man. He was paying for an evil life. Did his father now understand why he had wished him the fate of the poor man? Setna did.

Father and son spread their golden wings and flew swiftly back to Thebes. They re-entered their bodies and continued their ordinary lives, just as the sun began to rise.

Magic and Medicine

Magic was an important part of daily life. People used spells, incantations, and protective amulets to ward off illness or cure disorders. At the same time, ancient Egyptian physicians and healers were respected throughout the ancient world for their medical skills.

EARLY MEDICINE

Medicine in ancient Egypt was very advanced. Papyri have survived showing that early Egyptian doctors had a good understanding of anatomy, probably derived from embalming, and were able to recognize and diagnose a large number of illnesses. The so-called Ebers Papyrus, for instance, is a huge papyrus roll dating back to c. 1550 B.C.E. It lists various diseases, including eye and skin disorders and diseases relating to pregnancy. It also includes information about the body and more than 800 different treatments.

Right: A woman holds a bunch of lotus flowers. Plants and herbs were used in both magic and medicine. Then, as now, garlic was used for many complaints, particularly indigestion. Juniper berries were used to soothe chest pains and stomach cramps, and turmeric was used to close open wounds.

Above: Egyptian physicians carried out many surgical procedures. They treated brain disorders using a technique known as trepanning, which involved cutting a hole in the skull to release pressure. They did bone surgery and removed tumors. Surgical instruments included pincers, forceps, scissors, and saws. This relief at the Temple of Kom Ombo shows the entire range of a physician's tools.

RELIGIOUS TREATMENTS

Religion, magic, and medicine were closely related, so treatment for any disorder might include offerings to the gods, the use of spells, and herbs. Some priests were specially trained as doctors to treat the sick. Doctors used some techniques similar to those practiced today, such as listening to a pulse or tapping the back to check for respiratory problems. Doctors or official scribes kept medical records of diseases, diagnoses, and treatments, writing them on papyrus.

Above: Egyptians, alive or dead, wore charms and amulets to protect themselves against harm. The Wadjet eye, shown here, was considered to be the most powerful. The eye, thought to be the eye of Horus or of Ra, was flanked by the vulture goddess Nekhbet and the snake goddess, Wadjet.

Right: This court official was physician and dentist to Pharaoh Djoser. Poor teeth were common, perhaps because Egyptian bread was very gritty. Dentists filled teeth with a type of cement, used gold to hold loose teeth in place, and treated gum disease.

THE BLINDING OF TRUTH

> Ages ago there were two brothers: Truth and Falsehood. Truth was a handsome, trustworthy man, but Falsehood was devious and dishonest. He was jealous of his brother.

One day Truth borrowed a knife from his brother. It was a good knife with a flint blade and fine bone handle but nothing special. By accident he dropped it in the river. He told his brother and offered to replace it with a similar knife. But Falsehood refused, saying the knife was too valuable to replace. He insisted they take their dispute to a court of the gods.

TRUTH IS UNFAIRLY PUNISHED

Once in court before the gods, Falsehood claimed that his knife had been wonderful, with a copper blade as long as the Nile River and a magnificent handle carved from a hundred trees.

The gods accepted this, and Falsehood pressed home his claim. Truth admitted he had lost his brother's knife, so the court found in Falsehood's favor. As punishment, Falsehood insisted that his brother be blinded in both eyes and made to work in his house as a doorkeeper. The gods ordered that this be done.

After a while, Falsehood got tired of seeing his blind brother in his house. It made him uncomfortable. He summoned Truth's servants and told them to take their master into the desert where wild lions would kill him. The servants took Truth into the desert, but they let him escape. They returned to the house and told Falsehood that Truth was dead and they had seen him being eaten by a lion.

Truth wandered through the desert for many days. At last a woman caught sight of him and, because he was so handsome, took him to her home to be her doorkeeper. She was very attracted to Truth. Eventually she became pregnant with Truth's child. In due course she gave birth to a fine son. She did not tell her child the identity of his father.

MAAT: ORDER AND HARMONY

The Egyptians valued order and justice. The natural world could be unpredictable, although the universe—the movement of the sun, moon, and stars and the cycle of growing things—was known to be ordered and stable. The goddess Maat personified natural harmony and social order. Her name literally meant "truth," and she was worshipped throughout Egypt. Some Egyptologists have said that Maat was more of an idea or concept than a goddess because she stood for a universal stability, harmony, and balance. Egyptians believed that, without her, the world would descend into chaos. A pharaoh's task was to ensure social order and justice, and many took the title "Beloved of Maat" to emphasize that role. Some myths say that Maat was present when the universe was created, and she was believed to attend all judgments.

Right: The goddess Maat personified truth, order, and justice. She wore an ostrich feather, which symbolized truth. The hearts of the dead were weighed against her feather in the underworld.

Truth's son was handsome and wise like a god. He did well at school and the other students were jealous. They jeered at him and asked him why he did not have a father like other boys. The boy went home and asked his mother who his father was. To his amazement, she pointed at her doorkeeper.

TRUTH'S SON SEEKS REVENGE

The boy was overwhelmed with pity. He went to his father, hugged him, and prepared him a meal. He asked his father who had blinded him. Truth told his son the whole story—and there and then the boy decided to seek revenge for his father.

The son packed ten loaves of bread, a jug of water, a walking stick, and a sword. He took a magnificent ox from his mother's field and set out to Falsehood's farm. When he arrived he looked for the herdsman and asked him to guard his ox until he could return and collect it. As payment, the boy gave the herdsman the bread, water, stick, and sword.

Some while later, Falsehood passed by. Seeing the magnificent ox, he ordered the herdsman to kill it and prepare it for a fine meal. The herdsman refused, telling Falsehood that the ox belonged to someone else. Falsehood dismissed this and said the herdsman could replace it with another ox when the owner came back. Forced to obey his master, the herdsman agreed and Falsehood ate the ox.

The boy soon heard what had happened. He went straight to the herdsman and asked for his ox. Where was it? What had happened to it? The herdsman told him it had gone but offered the boy a replacement from Falsehood's herd. Naturally the boy, who had planned this carefully, refused, saying his ox was irreplaceable.

The boy insisted that Falsehood should appear in court before the gods, just as his father had. Standing in front of the gods, the boy stated that his ox had been the most magnificent ox in the world. He claimed it was so large that its tail would have touched the Nile Delta marshes and its horns would have reached the eastern and western mountains.

The gods started laughing, saying it was absolutely impossible for any ox to be that large. No ox could be the size of Egypt. Bravely the boy challenged the gods. Why did they not believe him? They had believed Falsehood's claim that the blade of his knife was as long as the Nile River. Was that possible?

This made the gods think. The boy continued. He accused Falsehood of lying and announced to the gods that he was Truth's son and had come to avenge his father. He asked the gods to choose between Truth and Falsehood. But Falsehood said the boy was

Above: This fragment of painting from the tomb of Nebamun, a sculptor and craftsman who worked on the royal tombs at Thebes, shows cattle being herded for inspection. The painting dates from c. 1390 B.C.E.

lying, as Truth was dead. He was so certain of this that he said, if Truth were found alive, he, Falsehood, should be blinded and made to work in Truth's house.

The boy fetched his father and the gods saw the truth. Falsehood was whipped, blinded, and made to work in Truth's house.

TIMELINE OF ANCIENT EGYPT

Historians organize ancient Egyptian history into dynasties, or groups, of kings. A third-century B.C.E. Egyptian historian called Manetho was the first to use this system. Dynasties are divided into Old, Middle, and New Kingdoms, with so-called Intermediate Periods in between when there was no strong central government.

c. 5500–3150 B.C.E. Pre-Dynastic Period

The Egyptians develop farming and settled communities. Two kingdoms emerge: Lower (North) and Upper (South) Egypt.

c. 3100–2686 B.C.E. Early Dynastic Period: First to Second Dynasties

Pharaoh Narmer (Menes) unifies Egypt with a capital at Memphis. The Egyptians develop hieroglyphs, a writing system that uses pictures and symbols.

c. 2890–2686 B.C.E.

Kings are buried in mastabas.

c. 2686–2181 B.C.E. Old Kingdom: Third to Eighth Dynasties

Kings are buried in the first true pyramids at Saqqara and Giza. Major gods include Atum and Ra, worshipped at Heliopolis. The cult of Osiris spreads.

c. 2670 B.C.E.

Pharaoh Djoser rules, and the step pyramid is built at Saqqara.

c. 2580 B.C.E.

The Great Pyramid is built at Giza for Pharaoh Khufu. It is the largest of the pyramids.

c. 2530 B.C.E.

The Great Sphinx is built at Giza during the reign of King Khafra.

c. 2350 B.C.E.

The first known Pyramid Texts are inscribed.

c. 2181–2055 B.C.E. First Intermediate Period: Ninth to Eleventh Dynasties

The pharaoh's power collapses. Two rulers govern Egypt from two cities: Memphis and Thebes.

c. 2055–c. 1650 B.C.E. Middle Kingdom: Eleventh to Fourteenth Dynasties

Egypt conquers Lower Nubia and trades with Syria and Palestine. The pyramid-building era draws to a close, while the first rock-cut tombs are built. Funeral customs spread from royalty to other social groups.

c. 1650–1550 B.C.E. Second Intermediate Period: Fifteenth to Seventeenth Dynasties

Hyksos kings from southwest Asia occupy the Nile Delta region and introduce horse-drawn chariots into Egypt. The Theban dynasty rules in the south.

c. 1550–1069 B.C.E. New Kingdom: Eighteenth to Twentieth Dynasties

Pharaohs rule Egypt again from Thebes. Egyptian civilization flourishes and reaches its greatest height.

c. 1550 B.C.E.

Royal tombs are built in the Valley of the Kings, western Thebes.

1545–1504 B.C.E.

Amenhotep I rules Egypt.

c. 1479 B.C.E.
Hatshepsut declares herself pharaoh.

c. 1390–1352 B.C.E.
Amenhotep III rules Egypt.

c. 1352–1336 B.C.E.
Akhenaten rules Egypt and bans all gods except the sun god Aten. He creates a new capital, Aten.

c. 1336 B.C.E.
The capital moves back to Memphis.

c. 1327 B.C.E.
Tutankhamun is buried in the Valley of the Kings.

c. 1279–1213 B.C.E.
Ramesses II, the Great, rules Egypt and introduces a huge building program of statues, monuments, and temples, including Abu Simbel.

c. 1274 B.C.E.
The Egyptians fight the Hittites at the Battle of Qadesh.

c. 1209 B.C.E.
Seafaring raiders from the Mediterranean, known as the Sea Peoples, threaten Egypt.

c. 1176 B.C.E.
Ramesses III defeats the Sea Peoples.

c. 1069–664 B.C.E. Third Intermediate Period: Twenty-first to Twenty-fifth Dynasties
Egyptian civilization declines, while Egypt divides into separate states.

c. 671 B.C.E.
Assyrians invade Egypt and reach Memphis.

c. 664–332 B.C.E. Late Period: Twenty-sixth to Thirty-first Dynasties

525 B.C.E.
Egypt becomes part of the Persian Empire.

404–343 B.C.E.
Egypt is independent again.

332 B.C.E.–395 C.E. Greco-Roman Period
Greeks and later Romans occupy Egypt. Christianity is introduced and the Egyptian gods disappear.

332–323 B.C.E.
Alexander the Great conquers Egypt, bringing it under Macedonian rule. Alexandria is founded.

305 B.C.E.
Ptolemy I of Macedonia assumes power, founding the Ptolemaic Dynasty.

30 B.C.E.
Egypt becomes part of the Roman Empire.

323 C.E.
Egypt adopts Christianity.

395 C.E.
Roman rule ends.

642 C.E.
The Arab conquest of Egypt leads to Egypt becoming a Muslim country.

GLOSSARY

amethyst Violet-blue type of quartz used as a gemstone.

amulet Magic charm, often a piece of jewelry, worn as protection against disease, evil spirits, or bad luck.

ankh Symbol of eternal life, shaped like a cross. Gods and pharaohs were often shown holding an *ankh*.

archaeologist A person who studies human cultures of the past through the analysis of architecture, artifacts, and other remains.

atef crown White crown of Lower Egypt.

ba A person's soul or spiritual aspect, often shown hovering over the mummified body of its owner.

canopic jars Containers that held the internal organs of a deceased person and were buried with the person.

consort Wife or husband of a ruler or god.

cult A system of religious worship or ritual.

Duat The underworld.

dynasty A succession of rulers all from the same family.

Egyptologist A person who studies ancient Egyptian history, architecture, and artifacts.

embalming Treating a dead body with a preserving substance so that it does not decay.

funerary rituals The rites that took place at funerals.

Heliopolis Capital of Egypt from c. 2780 to 2300 B.C.E.

Hermopolis A religious center dedicated to Thoth.

hieroglyphs The symbols that Egyptians used in their writing system. There were at least 700 different hieroglyphs, each corresponding to a sound or word.

ibis Heron-like wading bird with long legs and a curved beak.

inundation The annual Nile flood.

ka The life essence of a person. Egyptians believed the *ka* was a person's exact double and lived on after that person died.

lapis lazuli Bright blue gemstone.

malachite Bright green mineral.

mastaba Early Egyptian rectangular tomb.

Memphis The first capital of ancient Egypt c. 3100 B.C.E.

mortuary temple The place where the dead were prepared for burial and worshipped.

mummy An embalmed and wrapped corpse from ancient Egypt.

myrrh A scented gum obtained from a tree. It was highly prized in ancient Egypt and used in ointments and perfumes.

obelisk A stone pillar with tapering sides. Obelisks were carved with the titles of pharaohs and dedications to the gods.

ocher Reddish-colored or yellow earth used for dyes.

papyrus Marsh reed used to make paper and other items.

pharaoh Ancient Egyptian king. The word meant "great house."

Punt Ancient kingdom, probably on the east coast of Africa.

pylon A massive gateway.

scarab A sacred beetle modeled on the dung beetle, which lays its eggs in a ball of dung that it rolls along the ground.

scribe A person who kept written records on papyrus or stone.

senet A popular Egyptian board game.

Seven Hathors Seven cow goddesses who determined a child's destiny at birth.

shaduf A device for scooping up water.

stele (or stela) A stone slab decorated with inscriptions or reliefs.

syncretism The process by which ancient Egyptians merged gods.

tamarisk Evergreen shrub with masses of small flowers.

Thebes Capital of Egypt c. 1570 B.C.E., and center of Amun worship. Site of present-day Karnak and Luxor.

turmeric Bright yellow spice.

uraeus Royal emblem shaped like an attacking cobra.

vizier High official or adviser.

Wadjet (also udjat) The eye of Ra or Horus, a protective symbol.

FOR MORE INFORMATION

BOOKS

The following is a selection of books that have been used in the making of this volume, plus recommendations for further reading.

Andrews, Carol. *Egyptian Mummies*. Cambridge: Harvard University Press, 2004.

Armour, Robert A. *Gods and Myths of Ancient Egypt*. Cairo: American University in Cairo Press, 1986, 2001.

Gahlin, Lucia. *The Myths and Mythology of Ancient Egypt*. London: Southwater, 2003.

Hart, George. *Egyptian Myths: The Legendary Past*. Austin: University of Texas Press, 1990.

—. *Eyewitness Books: Ancient Egypt*. New York: DK Publishing, Inc., 2004.

—. *The Routledge Dictionary of Egyptian Gods and Goddesses*. New York: Taylor & Francis, 2005.

Lurker, Manfred. *An Illustrated Dictionary of the Gods and Symbols of Ancient Egypt*. London: Thames & Hudson, 1984.

Manley, Bill. *The Penguin Historical Atlas of Ancient Egypt*. New York: Penguin USA, 1997.

Morley, Jacqueline. *Egyptian Myths*. Grand Rapids: School Specialty Children's Publishing, 1999.

Nardo, Don. *Egyptian Mythology*. Berkeley Heights: Enslow, 2001.

Shaw, Ian, ed. *The Oxford History of Ancient Egypt*. Oxford: Oxford University Press, 2003.

Shaw, Ian, and Paul Nicholson. *The Dictionary of Ancient Egypt*. New York: Harry N. Abrams Inc., 2003.

Watterson, Barbara. *The Gods of Ancient Egypt*. New York: Sutton, 2003.

WEB SITES

www.ancientegypt.co.uk
A range of information, stories, and games on subjects such as daily life, mummification, trade, writing, pharaohs, the calendar, and pyramids.

www.egyptianmyths.net
Retellings of numerous myths, lists of gods and hieroglyphs, essays on different aspects of Egyptian life, and links to further resources.

www.nationalgeographic.com/pyramids
An interactive guide to the pyramids, plus stories about key Egyptian archaeological finds.

www.touregypt.net
A travel site with information on key archaeological sites, a hieroglyph converter, information on history and religion, recipes, and Egyptian news stories.

www.egyptologyonline.com
Information on fascinating aspects of ancient Egyptian life, such as pharaohs, religion, mummies, temples, and archaeology, plus extensive links.

MUSEUMS

Egyptian Museum, Cairo, Egypt
www.egyptianmuseum.gov.eg
The Egyptian Museum in Cairo houses over 120,000 objects ranging from prehistoric times to the Greco-Roman period. On display are objects from the tomb of Tutankhamun, a vast collection of mummies, jewelry, and sculpture.

British Museum, London, UK
www.thebritishmuseum.ac.uk/world/egypt/egypt.html
The Department of Ancient Egypt and Sudan has the largest collection of Egyptian antiquities outside Cairo, covering over 5,000 years of history. The displays include a gallery of monumental sculpture and a collection of mummies and coffins.

Metropolitan Museum of Art, New York, USA
www.metmuseum.org/works_of_Art/department.asp?dep=10
The collection of ancient Egyptian art at the Metropolitan Museum consists of approximately 36,000 objects of artistic, historical, and cultural importance. Fascinating displays include the Old Kingdom mastaba of Perneb (c. 2450 B.C.E.); jewelry belonging to Princess Sit-hathor-yunet of the Twelfth Dynasty; royal portrait sculpture dating from the Twelfth Dynasty; and statues of the female pharaoh Hatshepsut of the Eighteenth Dynasty.

INDEX

ACKNOWLEDGMENTS

Sources: AA = Art Archive **WFA** = Werner Forman Archive
AKG = akg-images **Scala** = Scala, Florence

b = bottom c = center t = top l = left r = right

Front cover: Corbis
Back cover: top Art Archive; **bottom** Corbis

Pages: 1 WFA, background AKG; **3** AA/Dagli Orti /Egyptian Museum, Turin; **7** Corbis/Jon Arnold/JAI; **8** WFA; **10** Corbis/Bojan Breclj; **13** WFA/Fitzwilliam Museum, Cambridge; **14** AA/Dagli Orti /Musée du Louvre, Paris; **15** WFA; **16-17** Bridgeman Art Library/British Museum, London; **18–19** AA/Dagli Orti /Ragab Papyrus Institute Cairo; **20r** AKG/ Herve Champollion; **20l** WFA/Schultz Collection, New York; **21r** AKG/ Musée du Louvre, Paris/Erich Lessing; **21b** AA/Dagli Orti /Musée du Louvre **23** Corbis/Sandro Vannini; **25** AKG/Nimatallah/Museo Archeologico, Florence; **27** AKG/Erich Lessing/Musee du Louvre;

28 WFA; **30** AKG/Erich Lessing/Musée du Louvre; **33** AKG/Erich Lessing; **35** WFA/Fitzwilliam Museum, Cambridge; **37** AA/Dagli Orti/ Musée du Louvre; **38** AKG/Francois Guenet; **39** AA/Dagli Orti; **40t** Scala/Egyptian Museum, Vatican City; **40b** WFA/E. Strouhal; **41t** AKG/Erich Lessing /National Maritime Museum, Haifa; **41b** Scala/ Egyptian Museum, Berlin; **43–45** WFA; **46** Corbis/Roger Wood; **49** Corbis/Charles & Josette Lenars; **50** WFA/Egyptian Museum, Cairo; **53** AKG/Erich Lessing /Musee du Louvre; **54–55** AKG/Erich Lessing; **56t & b** AKG/Herve Champollion; **57t&b** AA/Dagli Orti; **59** Corbis/ Jose Fuste Raga; **60** WFA; **61** WFA/E.Strouhal; **63** AKG/Erich Lessing; **65** Corbis/Roger Wood; **67** WFA; **68t** WFA/Egyptian Museum, Cairo; **68b** AKG/Erich Lessing; **70** WFA/Egyptian Museum, Cairo; **73** AA/ Eileen Tweedy/ British Museum, London; **74** Corbis/Gianni Dagli Orti; **77–78** WFA/Egyptian Museum, Cairo; **81** Getty Images/Kenneth Garrett; **82** AA/Jacqueline Hyde/British Museum, London; **84t** AA/Dagli Orti; **84b** WFA/ British Museum, London; **85l & r** WFA/Egyptian Museum, Cairo; **87** Scala/Museo Archeologico, Florence; **89** WFA/British Museum, London